BIBLE BASICS
Finding Tools to Read and Interpret Scripture

Donald W. Patterson

Northwestern Publishing House
Milwaukee, Wisconsin

Second printing, 2013

Cover illustrations: Lars Justinen; GoodSalt, Inc.
Art Director: Karen Knutson
Designer: Pamela Dunn

All Scripture is taken from the HOLY BIBLE, NEW INTERNATIONAL VERSION®. NIV®. Copyright © 1973, 1978, 1984 by Biblica, Inc.™ Used by permission of Zondervan. All rights reserved worldwide.

All rights reserved. This publication may not be copied, photocopied, reproduced, translated, or converted to any electronic or machine-readable form in whole or in part, except for brief quotations, without prior written approval from the publisher.

Northwestern Publishing House
1250 N. 113th St., Milwaukee, WI 53226-3284
www.nph.net
© 2010 by Northwestern Publishing House
Published 2010
Printed in the United States of America
ISBN 978-0-8100-2269-0

Table of Contents

Introduction 5

One
A Simple Introduction to the Bible........................... 9

Two
What Does the Bible Say About Itself?...................... 15

Three
The Story of the Old Testament 27

Four
The Story of the New Testament............................ 47

Five
Learning to Properly Interpret and Apply the Bible 67

Six
Styles of Literature Found in the Bible...................... 85

Seven
Ways to Approach the Bible 92

Introduction

Swimming in the Bible

For some people, reading the Bible is like being around a swimming pool. They are very cautious. After all, too many people have drowned in those things. One time I saw a rowdy crowd by a backyard pool. One by one the people in the crowd were tossing people in. When they grabbed one lady, she started screaming, "No, no! I can't swim!" Thankfully they let her go. She wanted nothing to do with that pool.

That's how a lot of people feel about the Bible. They squirm whenever anyone pushes them close to a Bible. If they are invited to read it or study it, they get that look on their faces that says, "No, no! I can't swim!"

Others shy away from the Bible because it seems irrelevant. All they have ever read in the Bible were stories from faraway places, which took place at a time that seems to have nothing to do with the here and now. Or they have read poems that didn't make any sense to them or have come across lists of names that went on for chapters.

For others the Bible seems weird. Weird people have used the Bible to intimidate and bully them. They've had Bible "bullets" shot at them left and right by people trying to convert them to their way of thinking, without taking the time to gently teach them what they need to know. Seeing people on the corner of big city streets with grocery baskets and bull horns shouting out Bible verses at passersby hasn't helped their perception of the Bible either.

Still others are frightened by the Bible because they have heard of people doing scary and mean things, claiming the Bible led them to do those things. They think of cult leaders like Jim Jones and David Koresh. The ancient crusades and abortion clinic bombings have been justified by the Bible. If the Bible leads people to act in those ways, people reason, they want nothing to do with it.

The simple truth is that most people who shy away from the Bible have never really learned how to read it properly. The Bible is the most wonderful book on this planet. When you read it, you touch the heart of God. It answers all the big questions we have in life: such as, How did we get here? Why were we put here? Where are we going? How do we make the most out of our lives? And what happens after we die?

Although some find the Bible difficult to read, you can't escape the fact that the Bible is the all-time best seller as well as the most studied and revered book of all time. Government leaders have sometimes tried to eradicate the Bible from their nations because it garnered more loyalty than they ever could. The harder they tried to suppress it, the more it was printed and studied. That's because it is God's book. And God wants to give it to the world. It reveals God to us, and God will stop at nothing to have himself revealed. He made us, and he wants us to be in his family. That's why he gave us the Bible.

Have you wanted to take a "swim" in the Bible but held back because you were not sure where the shallow end was? The Bible has many books with difficult-to-pronounce names and different writing styles. Where is a person supposed to start?

The way to start is with a proper introduction. That's where this book comes in. It will properly introduce you to the Bible. And I am excited to be your greeter, because no book even comes close to the Bible's message, its power, and its ability to renew the human heart. We will start at the shallow end, with the basics, and then move out into deeper waters. Take your time, and work on understanding what you are reading.

If you read this book carefully, by the end you should be able to read the Bible at any time, starting in any place, and enjoy what it has to offer.

If you don't have your own copy of the Bible, I urge you to go out and get one. You will want to use it while you are reading this book. If I were teaching you how to swim, we would be at a pool. If you are to learn how to get around in the Bible, you have to be near a

Bible. I recommend that you get a New International Version (NIV) of the Bible. It is easy to read, and it fairly accurately translates the meaning of the original Bible. All Bible quotes in *Bible Basics* come from the NIV. Using the same version will make it easier for you.

Bible References

Throughout this book you will see Bible references, for example, Genesis 1:1. The word *Genesis* refers to the book of the Bible where the passage is found. The number before the colon is the chapter in which you find the verse. The number after the colon is the verse within that chapter.

Definitions

Here are a few definitions of terms you will find as you read this book and when you jump into your Bible.

Apostle—A man who was sent by Jesus to tell the world that Jesus had come as our Savior. There are 13 apostles in the New Testament. Twelve of those men lived with Jesus and saw all the events of his ministry. The 13th was a man named Paul, whom Jesus called to be an apostle after Jesus had ascended into heaven. God called the apostles to bear witness to Jesus' resurrection, and he inspired them to write and teach his Word.

Christ—The New Testament translation of the Old Testament word *messiah*. It means the "Anointed One." Some people think that Christ was Jesus' last name. His last name was Bar-Joseph. But since he was the long-promised "Anointed One," he bears the title "Christ" after his name. To *anoint* someone is to set that person apart for a special task. Jesus was set apart by God to win our salvation.

Disciple—A follower of Jesus. Christians today are sometimes called disciples too. Jesus had many disciples. He chose 12 of them to receive special training and attention. He set them aside to be the 12 apostles.

Holy Land—In the Bible it is also called the Promised Land. This is a term used for the land that God promised to give to Abraham and his descendants, who were called the people of Israel. It is also where Jesus lived and worked. Today this land is considered holy by three religions: Islam, Christianity, and Judaism.

Israel—This is the name that the Bible uses for God's chosen people. It comes from the name of one of their forefathers. At first the name of this man was Jacob, but very early in the Bible (Genesis 32:28) he was renamed Israel.

Jews—By New Testament times, the Israelites were most often called Jews. This name is derived from *Judah,* one of the 12 tribes into which the Israelites were divided and the only tribe still in existence when Jesus was born.

Prophet—Someone that God sent to tell his people what was on his mind about their past, present, or future. Seventeen books of the Bible were written by prophets. Most prophets appear in the Old Testament, but there are also a few in the New Testament.

Messiah—This is an Old Testament word that means the "Anointed One." The New Testament word for Messiah is *Christ.*

A Simple Introduction to the Bible

One day my son's high school classmate challenged him with these questions: "Isn't the Bible just like the Koran of Islam and the books that the Buddhists follow? They're all old books that teach old religions, aren't they?" My son's friend is not alone in his view of the Bible. The books he mentioned were all written long before we were born. They're all believed to be the authoritative word of God. And they all talk about God and people. But that is pretty much the extent of their similarities.

There are important differences between the Bible and other holy books. First of all, the Bible is a much older book than either the Koran or the teachings of Buddha. Consider this: The entire Bible was finished in A.D. 95. That's about five hundred years before the Koran was written. The teachings of Buddha were not actually written down until around 100 B.C. More than two-thirds of the Bible was completed by that time, and the very first books of the Bible were written 1,300 years before any Buddhist scriptures even existed. So, the Bible has been around much longer than either the Koran or the writings of Buddha.

Another difference is the amazing continuity in the Bible. It was written by more than 50 people whose lives spanned more than 1,500 years. Most of its authors never met one another and yet their writings have a consistent message that develops slowly and carefully throughout their collective work. In other words, the Bible is a collection of writings from God, sent through more than 50 different men, that tells a single story that unfolds over a 1,500–year period. No other collection of books in this world has such diverse origins and yet such continuity and singular purpose! Compare that to the Koran and the teachings of Buddha. One man wrote the Koran over a very short period of time. The teachings of Buddha are largely the work of one man as well and were committed to memory by monks for three hundred years before they ever started writing them down.

However, the greatest difference between the Bible and other religious holy books is not who wrote them or how long it took. The greatest difference is their message. The Bible tells how God reached down to save all people for eternal life. No other book teaches that! The Koran, the teachings of Buddha, and all other religious holy books tell how people must save themselves by working their way up to God. The only holy book that tells us about a God who came down to us and saved us is the Bible. That's a huge difference!

A Brief Overview of the Bible

The Bible is a single book. But it is also a collection of many different writings. To keep it simple, we call those writings books, but actually only some of them read like a book with a story line that goes from beginning to end. Others are collections of poetry and ancient prophecy. Some are even letters from one person to another or to a group of people. The best way to get to know which books are prose and which are not is by reading the Bible slowly and carefully with study helps. For the moment, keep in mind that there are 66 books in the Bible and that some of the books are telling stories while others are poetry and letters.

Old Testament Overview

The Bible is divided into two main collections. The first collection of 39 books is called the Old Testament. This section of the Bible was originally written in Hebrew. Moses wrote the first five books of the Old Testament around 1500 B.C. The last book of the Old Testament was written by a prophet named Malachi around 430 B.C. One can easily divide the Old Testament into three main sections: history, poetry, and prophecy.

The first section of the Old Testament is a collection of 17 *historical books.* They run from Genesis to Esther. Each of these books is a historical narrative. As a whole, they tell the story of how God created the universe, the earth, and everything in it. They tell how God made human beings the crown of his creation and how the first people fell away from God. God's response to the first people's sin was to forestall his just punishment and promise a Savior who would reconcile the world to himself.

As history unfolded, God kept expanding his promise to send a Savior. God's promises of a coming Savior appear in the fabric of the very real history of humankind and especially of God's own people called the Israelites. If you want to start "swimming" in the Old Testament of the Bible, you need to read the historical books first. They are the shallow end of the pool. Chapter 3 of *Bible Basics* has a historical summary of the Old Testament. Reading that chapter will give you a birds-eye view of the Old Testament historical books. The rest of the Old Testament books (the books of poetry and prophecy) were written during the time covered by the historical books.

The second set of books in the Old Testament is the *poetical books*. This section contains the five books from Job to Song of Songs. These writings are mostly wisdom literature put into ancient Hebrew poetic forms. They are good for meditation and counsel in godly living. One of them, the book of Psalms, was the song book of the ancient Israelites. In a predominantly oral society, these psalms were very valuable teaching tools because people memorized them and sang them regularly.

Below is a table of contents for the Old Testament organized into three divisions.

Historical Books	Genesis, Exodus, Leviticus, Numbers, Deuteronomy, Joshua, Judges, Ruth, 1 Samuel, 2 Samuel, 1 Kings, 2 Kings, 1 Chronicles, 2 Chronicles, Ezra, Nehemiah, Esther
Poetical Books	Job, Psalms, Proverbs, Ecclesiastes, Song of Songs
Prophetic Books	Isaiah, Jeremiah, Lamentations, Ezekiel, Daniel, Hosea, Joel, Amos, Obadiah, Jonah, Micah, Nahum, Habakkuk, Zephaniah, Haggai, Zechariah, Malachi

The third set of books in the Old Testament is the *prophetic books*. This is a collection of 17 prophetic works. Each book is named after the man who wrote it. This section contains the books from Isaiah to Malachi. The prophets were commissioned by God to tell his people what was on God's mind about their past, present, and future. These books are written mostly in poetry and are sprinkled with prophecies about the coming Savior. Chapter 53 of Isaiah gives amazing detail about the crucifixion and resurrection of Jesus Christ. It was written approximately seven hundred years before he was born!

Maybe you are wondering where the name *Old Testament* came from. The word *testament* means "a formal agreement." People call the first 39 books of the Bible the Old *Testament* because in these historical books, God made a formal agreement with his people, the Israelites, that he would be their God if they would follow all of the laws that he gave them from Mount Sinai. You can find the giving of that Law in Exodus chapters 20–23.

The phrase *Old Testament* was coined by Christians because 480 years after the books of the Old Testament were finished, God inspired men to write the second major section of the Bible. We call it the New Testament because in these books we learn about how God fulfilled his promise to Adam and Eve and made a new covenant of peace between him and the world through Jesus' sacrifice for us.

New Testament Overview

In the New Testament we see that God sent Jesus Christ to be the Savior of the world! Through Jesus he made a new formal agreement with all people. He agreed to forgive all our sins, forever. Not a bad agreement, is it? The New Testament is a collection of 27 books that were originally written in Greek. Together they form about one-third of the entire Bible. The first book of the New Testament was written around A.D. 40 and the last around A.D. 95. You can easily divide the New Testament into three sections: history, letters, and prophecy.

There are five *historical books* in the New Testament. The first four books (Matthew, Mark, Luke, and John) tell the story of the life of

Jesus Christ. He is the Savior that was long promised in the Old Testament. These four books tell the same story, but they were written by four different authors to four slightly different original audiences. The four books work together nicely to tell us all we need to know about our Savior Jesus Christ. If the Bible were a mountain range, then these books would form the tallest peak.

If you are going to meet God in the Bible, you simply must read these books. In them God shows us who he is and what he has done for us in Jesus Christ. We call them the four gospels. The word *gospel* means "good news." These books tell the good news of how God loves us and how he has saved us in Jesus Christ! If you have never read them, make that your first goal in getting to know the Bible. You can finish them easily in four weeks by reading one book each week. Just as I said about the historical books of the Old Testament, the four gospels are the shallow end of the pool in the New Testament. Chapter 5 of *Bible Basics* is a summary of the New Testament history. Reading it before you start reading the actual New Testament will help you get acquainted with the story line before delving into the New Testament itself.

The book of Acts, is the fifth historical book. It tells us how the first followers of Jesus spread his Word far and wide. As you read Acts you will see how churches popped up all over the Mediterranean world as Christians spread the good news about Jesus! The main characters are the apostles Peter and Paul, the first two prominent leaders of the Christian faith.

After the book of Acts, you will find 21 *letters* written by Christian leaders to either churches or individuals. These letters give us tremendous insights about the Christian life that God has given us. You'll want to read them again and again to learn what it means to be a Christian.

The last book of the Bible is Revelation. It is the lone *prophetic book* of the New Testament. In this book you will find many fantastic visions that were given to John, a prominent early apostle and Christian leader. These visions show us how God is guiding all world history to a very definite conclusion—when he will finally take all of his followers to heaven. There we will spend eternity with him in everlasting joy. It is a very comforting book if you understand it properly. If you are just now getting acquainted with the Bible, please wait until you have read and understood the rest of the Bible before you delve into Revelation. It is the deep end of the pool. Before you venture out there, you need to learn to swim well. Below is a table of contents for the New Testament organized into the three divisions.

Historical Books	Matthew, Mark, Luke, John, Acts
Letters	Romans, 1 Corinthians. 2 Corinthians, Galatians, Ephesians, Philippians, Colossians, 1 Thessalonians, 2 Thessalonians, 1 Timothy, 2 Timothy, Titus, Philemon, Hebrews, James, 1 Peter, 2 Peter, 1 John, 2 John, 3 John, Jude
Prophetic Book	Revelation

There is no other book in the world like the Bible. Even though it was written by more than 50 authors and it took more than 1,500 years to finish, its message is the same from beginning to end: God loves all people and sent his Son, Jesus, to save us. The Bible has 66 books divided into two main sections: the Old and New Testaments. The Old Testament was written in Hebrew and was finished in 430 B.C. The New Testament was written in Greek and was finished in A.D. 95. If you have not read the Bible before, it is best to read the first 17 books of Old Testament and then the first 5 books of the New Testament. These are the historical books of the Bible. The rest of the books will make more sense if you familiarize yourself with the historical books first.

What Does the Bible Say About Itself?

Not too long ago someone introduced me to his very dear friend. He told me all about him while his friend just stood there and politely smiled. Then our mutual friend was drawn away by a phone call. He left us standing together. I was glad it happened. Now his friend could speak for himself. He told me all about his upbringing, his family, his hobbies, and his goals in life. I really got to know him well as he talked for himself.

So far I have simply introduced you to the Bible. It's time for me to let the Bible speak for itself. Once you have learned what it has to say about itself, you will feel much better acquainted with it.

The Bible Is the Word of God

First of all, the Bible tells us that it is the very Word of God. For instance, there is a book in the Old Testament called Isaiah. Isaiah the prophet lived around 700 B.C. God had given Isaiah many prophecies about the things God was going to do for his people, the Israelites. But not many Israelites were listening to Isaiah. Instead, they were going to witches and warlocks to find "truth." Isaiah firmly rebuked the Israelites. In his rebuke he told them that if the witches and warlocks did not speak the words God had given him, then they were unable to tell the truth about the future at all. Isaiah said that they had "no light of dawn" in them.

Isaiah said this about the Word that God had given him:

> *The LORD spoke to me with his strong hand upon me,* warning me not to follow the way of this people. . . . When men tell you to consult mediums and spiritists, who whisper and mutter, should not a people inquire of their God? Why consult the dead on behalf of the living? *To the law and to the testimony! If they do not speak according to this word, they have no light of dawn.* (Isaiah 8:11,19,20)

15

Isaiah said that God spoke to him with his strong hand upon him and gave him the words he was to speak. Then he mentioned the "law" and "the testimony." He was referring to the prophecies that he had been given for the people. Isaiah had told the people to bind up his scrolls and save them until God made his words come true. His prophecies came true in the history of Israel and later in the life of Jesus Christ. Some of them are yet to be fulfilled in heaven. Isaiah's prophecies came true because they are the Word of God. That's what Isaiah was claiming!

This little example of what the Bible says about itself is duplicated hundreds of times over in all the prophetic writings of the Old Testament. Time and time again the prophets said, "This is what God said to me," or "The Word of the Lord says," or "Thus says the Lord!" These men knew they were sent by God. The message burned inside of them. They had to tell it. And we are glad they did, because we find in their messages everything God wants us to know about himself and the relationship he has established with us.

Not only did the biblical authors of the Old Testament say they themselves were writing the Word of God, they said the other authors were too! You have to remember that the Old Testament was written over a period of a thousand years. That means that many of its authors had access to previously written Old Testament books. The later authors testified that the Word of God written before them was the very Word of God. Consider Psalm 1. It is attributed to David. He was speaking about the first five books of the Bible when he said:

> Blessed is the man
> who does not walk in the counsel of the wicked
> or stand in the way of sinners
> or sit in the seat of mockers.
>
> But his delight is in *the law of the* LORD,
> and *on his law* he meditates day and night. (Psalm 1:1,2)

For David, the words of Moses were the very words of God. The word *law* is the translation of the Hebrew word *torah*. Very often the word *law* refers to the first five books of the Bible written by Moses. Often a psalmist used the word *law* to refer to all of the books of the Bible that were written up to that point. Either way, you can easily see that David was saying that the other books of the Bible are God's Word.

David said that he meditated on God's laws, letting them guide him into godly living. Psalm 119 is the longest chapter in the Bible. It is one very long tribute to all the Scriptures that came before. The Scriptures are the wonderful words of God. Many Christians can recite verse 105. Referring to all the previous writings of Scripture as the Word of God, it says, "Your word is a lamp to my feet and a light for my path."

The New Testament authors also proclaimed that the Old Testament is the very Word of God. The clearest and boldest claim is found in a letter written by the apostle Paul. He was one of the first Christian missionaries. In one of his letters called 2 Timothy, he says this about God's Word:

> As for you, continue in what you have learned and have become convinced of, because you know those from whom you learned it, and how from infancy you have known the holy Scriptures, which are able to make you wise for salvation through faith in Christ Jesus. *All Scripture is God-breathed* and is useful for teaching, rebuking, correcting and training in righteousness, so that the man of God may be thoroughly equipped for every good work. (2 Timothy 3:14-17)

When Paul wrote these words, he feared that he would soon die under Roman persecution, so he encouraged Timothy to keep reading the Old Testament after he was gone. He wanted Timothy to stay in the true faith by reading God's Word. "All Scripture is God-breathed." You can't get any bolder and clearer about the Holy Scriptures than that!

Paul wasn't the only one to call the Old Testament the Word of God. As you read through the New Testament and especially through the four gospels, you will notice that Jesus and the apostles often referred to the entire Old Testament as the very Word of God. (For examples, see John 10:35; 2 Timothy 2:15; 1 Peter 1:10-12; and 2 Peter 3:16.)

But can the same claim be made about the New Testament? It can. In his letter called 1 Thessalonians, the apostle Paul commended the people for accepting his teachings as the Word of God. Here's how he said it:

> And we also thank God continually because, *when you received the word of God, which you heard from us,* you accepted it not as the word of men, but *as it actually is, the word of God,* which is at work in you who believe. (1 Thessalonians 2:13)

Jesus told his apostles that after he ascended into heaven, he would send the Holy Spirit to guide them into all truth. Jesus said, "But when he, the Spirit of truth, comes, *he will guide you into all truth.* He will not speak on his own; he will speak only what he hears, and he will tell you what is yet to come" (John 16:13). Jesus sent his Holy Spirit to the apostles on the great day of Pentecost (Acts 2), and from that day forward, they spoke and wrote the words of God as the Holy Spirit led them. There are several other places in the New Testament where the authors claimed that they were writing and teaching the Word of God. (See 1 Corinthians 2:4,5; Hebrews 4:12; Ephesians 6:17; Acts 6:4; James 1:22.)

Peter put the writings of Paul on the same level as the Old Testament when he wrote in 2 Peter 3:15,16:

> Bear in mind that our Lord's patience means salvation, just as our dear brother *Paul also wrote you with the wisdom that God gave him.* He writes the same way in all his letters, speaking in them of these matters. His letters contain some things that are hard to understand, which ignorant and unstable people distort, *as they do the other Scriptures,* to their own destruction.

Peter called Paul's writings "the wisdom that God gave him," and he said they were twisted like the "other Scriptures," meaning the Old Testament. For Peter, Paul's writings were the Word of God.

The Bible claims to be the Word of God from beginning to end! That's pretty bold, isn't it? It's very bold! It's a claim that is hard for a lot of people to accept. Other books claim to be the Word of God too. How can we know the Bible really is the Word of God? Well, consider a few more facts.

The Bible Did Not Originate in the Minds of People

If you study the origin of most other esteemed "holy" books, you will find that their authors set out to be spiritual gurus long before they wrote down their words. That really isn't true of the Bible writers. Most of the biblical authors spoke or wrote the Word of God irrespective of their desire to do so. This makes the Bible unique. Here is a verse from a letter in the New Testament called 2 Peter. Peter was one of the original 12 apostles. Peter believed he would soon be executed when he wrote these words, so he was bolstering Christians' trust in the Bible for after he was gone.

> We did not follow cleverly invented stories when we told you about the power and coming of our Lord Jesus Christ, but we were eyewitnesses of his majesty. For he received honor and glory from God the Father when the voice came to him from the Majestic Glory, saying, "This is my Son, whom I love; with him I am well pleased." We ourselves heard this voice that came from heaven when we were with him on the sacred mountain.
>
> And we have the word of the prophets made more certain, and you will do well to pay attention to it, as to a light shining in a dark place, until the day dawns and the morning star rises in your hearts. Above all, you must understand that no prophecy of Scripture came about by the prophet's own interpretation. *For prophecy never had its origin in the will of man, but men spoke from God as they were carried along by the Holy Spirit.* (2 Peter 1:16-21)

In the first paragraph, Peter in effect says, "Hey, we apostles didn't make all this up in our heads. We saw Jesus shining with God's glory on the mountain, and we heard the voice of the heavenly Father when we were there. These stories didn't come *from* us. They came *to* us!" Peter was about to die for his faith in God, who had revealed himself in Jesus. He was being persecuted for telling the truth. He wasn't about to let himself die for something he had invented. And he didn't want us to think that he had invented it!

In the second paragraph, Peter turns to the Old Testament prophets. He says that they too are set apart from all other religious writers. To paraphrase what he said: "Their writings did not originate with them. Their words were not their own interpretations of the times in which they lived." Read the last sentence again slowly and carefully: "For prophecy never had its origin in the will of man, but men spoke from God as they were carried along by the Holy Spirit." Prophecy never had its origin in the will of men. By that Peter means that the Old Testament writers didn't necessarily *want* to say or write Holy Scripture. Instead, God took over their minds and wills and drove them to it.

You can actually see what Peter is saying when you page through the Old Testament. Take the prophet Moses as an example. He didn't want to be a prophet. In Exodus chapters 3 and 4 we are told that Moses resisted God in several different ways before God commanded Moses against his will to go and speak for him.

Joseph and Daniel were two Old Testament men who by God's power could interpret dreams. Both of them claimed that they had no power in themselves to do so. They had to wait on God to give them the answers.

Open your Bible to 1 Samuel chapter 3. Samuel was a great prophet of God's Israelites. When Samuel was a little boy, he was raised by the Jewish high priest Eli. Samuel's mother took him to live with Eli when Samuel was only three. She was fulfilling her vow to God. One night when Samuel was still a boy, God awakened him and called him into service. Samuel wasn't seeking the prophetic ministry. Instead, God chose him.

King David was another Bible writer God called into his service. As a boy he killed a giant named Goliath. David was out watching sheep when God sent Samuel to anoint him to be the next king. After he was anointed, David also began to be used by God as his spokesman. He would go on to write almost half of the psalms. Like the others, he didn't call himself to be a prophet. God did.

Isaiah wrote one of the largest books in the Old Testament. In chapter 6 of his book, we discover that he also was appointed by God to be a prophet. Isaiah didn't appoint himself.

Another prophet, Jeremiah, was called before he was born. He never had a chance to refuse. He did entertain thoughts of quitting, but he said that God wouldn't let him quit (Jeremiah 20:9).

Another man, Elijah, tried to quit too, but God turned him around and marched him back into service. Then God sent Elijah to a surprised Elisha, who was plowing a field with 12 yoke of oxen. Elijah walked up to Elisha without forewarning and threw his cloak around him to mark him as the next prophet. Elisha didn't pursue the office. It pursued him.

Perhaps the best example of a reluctant prophet was Jonah. He ran the other way when God called him to preach to the city of Ninevah and ended up inside a giant fish for three days. This impressed on him that he could not refuse God's call.

Amos, another Old Testament prophet, defended himself when he was criticized for prophesying gloom and doom. To paraphrase his words: "I was a shepherd and tended grapevines when God tapped me on the shoulder and told me to come to Israel and say the things I have been saying." Again, God called Amos to preach his Word irrespective of Amos' will.

Even Peter himself was a reluctant servant of Jesus at first. And the last apostle, Paul, Jesus stopped dead in his tracks while chasing down Christians to put them to death. One biblical author after another was called to write for God either against his own will or irrespective of it. No other book has that kind of track record. How true Peter's words are: "Prophecy never had its origin in the will of man."

Maybe you have had a hard time trusting the Bible as God's Word because you haven't trusted people. But think about it! These men did not create the Bible. God created it through them. They were so overwhelmed that they had to write and speak. One time, when Peter was put on trial for telling others about Jesus, he said, "We cannot help speaking about what we have seen and heard" (Acts 4:20). That pretty much sums up reality for every biblical author! God wrote and spoke through them without asking their permission!

The Men Who Wrote the Bible Gave Their Lives for What They Wrote

Do you think if the 50-plus men who wrote the Bible were just making these things up, that so many of them would have given their lives for what they knew was a lie? But in the Old and New Testaments alike, one by one they were martyred for being God's messengers. Others, like Moses, didn't die at the hands of people for speaking the Word of God, but he chose the hard life of leading malcontents out into the wilderness because of the call God had given him. He knew God was serious. And later he carefully wrote the words that God gave to him, no matter how the Israelites treated those words.

Isaiah wrote and preached God's Word even though from the outset God had told him not many would listen to him. He took God at his word no matter the cost. On one occasion, God turned Ezekiel into an object lesson. God did not let the prophet Ezekiel outwardly mourn the death of his wife (Ezekiel 24:16). The prophet Hosea had to marry a prostitute to illustrate something to the Israelites. Jeremiah got into all kinds of trouble for telling people what God wanted. He was abused, and persecuted, and finally had to flee to Egypt along with God's people, where he died. Elijah had to experience a 3½-year drought and live under the queen's death sentence after he cleansed the land of false prophets and priests.

John the Baptist in the New Testament was killed for faithfully preaching the Word of God. All of the apostles in the New Testament were abused and persecuted and finally martyred for the Word of God, except for the apostle John. He was banished to the island of Patmos for testifying about Jesus Christ. All these men suffered dearly for what they preached and wrote. So why did they keep on preaching and writing? There is only one answer. They knew beyond all doubt that God was speaking and writing through them. They wouldn't get in his way. They had the truth from heaven, and they knew it!

The Bible Has More Prophecy and Fulfillment Than Any Other Book

One of the most convincing proofs that the Bible is the Word of God is the Bible's track record of prophecy and fulfillment. The Old Testament was completed around 430 B.C. Many Jews studied it and copied it for themselves. Around 250 B.C. the Old Testament was translated into Greek by Jewish authorities. The point is this: The Old Testament with all of its many prophecies was in existence for hundreds of years before Jesus was born.

In the passages of the Old Testament, you find many specific prophecies about the coming Messiah.

When we read the gospels, we see how God began fulfilling one prophecy after another. God chose a young Jewish virgin, Mary, to fulfill his promise that Jesus would be born of a virgin. He moved the Roman caesar to call for a census of the entire world in order to ensure that Jesus was born in Bethlehem. He made the Romans crucify two criminals alongside Jesus so that Isaiah's words, "he was assigned a grave with the wicked," would come true (Isaiah 53:9). Then he had Joseph of Arimathea bury Jesus in his own family grave so that the rest of Isaiah's prophecy would also come true: "[A grave] with the rich in his death."

Now remember, there are more than 60 major prophecies about Jesus in the Old Testament, and every one of them was fulfilled in his lifetime. Humanly speaking, the odds of this happening are astronomical. One person put it this way. Imagine a person spreading silver dollars over the state of Texas two feet deep. Then he would mark an X on just one of them, toss it anywhere in the state, and then thoroughly mix all the coins. Then he would blindfold a man and tell him he had one chance to randomly pick that one marked silver dollar. The odds of the blindfolded man choosing that one coin in only one try are the same as the odds that eight of the messianic prophecies could have coincidentally been fulfilled in the life of one man. Consider how many people were involved in the fulfillment of 60 prophecies, all of these people acting in concert even while completely unaware of what they were doing. Only God could have pulled this off. No other religious book can compare. The Bible is God's Word! There really is no other conclusion we can come to.

The Bible's Main Message Is About Jesus Christ

One time a member of my church came into my study very excited. He had discovered a book in the grocery store that said the Bible has many secret messages encoded in the original languages. The author had counted the many letters found in the Bible and had created systems of analyzing the text. His systems had formulas for choosing a letter from this or that word and for forming new words and messages from these letters. When he applied his formulas to passages of Scripture, they gave new messages that were very different from the original Scripture verses. The author proposed that God had hidden many messages in the outward forms of the Bible.

But that is not how God intended anyone to read the Bible. My friend was deflated when I told him that his book was a hoax. God hasn't hidden anything in the Bible. It is all there in plain language.

This is a gross example of how some people distort the message of the Bible. A more common mistake happens when people take a passage from here and another from there and piece together their own ideas about what messages they see in the Word. In fact, some of the most popular Bible teachers are guilty of such distortions.

The key to understanding the Bible lies in the old saying: "The main thing is that you keep the main thing, the main thing!" What is the main thing? You have to read the whole story to find out.

Look at John chapter 5. There we find Jesus discussing the Old Testament with men called scribes. They were the greatest Old Testament experts on the planet. And yet, because they emphasized the laws of Scripture, they missed the main thing! Listen to what Jesus said to them: "You diligently study the Scriptures because you think that by them you possess eternal life. These are the Scriptures that testify about me, yet you refuse to come to me to have life" (John 5:39,40). What was the main thing the scribes were missing? It was Jesus! Jesus is the main message of the Bible.

From the very beginning, when God first promised to send a Savior, to the very end, the whole book is about Jesus Christ. (Also see John 4:25,26; Romans 1:2,3; Romans 2; and Revelation 19:10.) We are happy that he is the main message because Jesus meets our greatest need. Our greatest need is not to have more money or fewer problems in life. Our greatest need is to escape what will happen if we die without Jesus. Satan has led us into sin. And sin has brought the threat of eternal death into our lives. But God promised to send his own Son, who would die for the sins of the world. Jesus was that man, born according to prophecy from a real mother, having been miraculously conceived by God. He never sinned during his entire 33-year life. And then, at the end of his life, Jesus took on himself the just wrath of God for our sins and overcame death for us. He rose from the dead to tell us that our sins were paid for and that we will go to heaven when we die if we trust in him.

This is the main thing that Jesus was talking about to a group of Jewish religious leaders when he said, "These are the Scriptures that testify about me, yet you refuse to come to me to have life" (John 5:39,40). We don't want to be like those people who refused to come to Jesus. When we read the Bible, we want to see Jesus on every page, come to him in faith, and enjoy the life he promises us. Through him, we too will overcome death and have eternal life. Jesus has saved us! That is the main message of God's Word!

God wants us to learn many things from his Word. He wants us to learn how to live in line with his will. He wants us to learn about the people and the places in the Bible. He wants us to learn about prayer and worship and parenting and many more things. But above all, he wants us to learn and keep learning that he loves us so much he sacrificed his own Son for us so that we could be saved and have an eternal relationship with him. The main thing in studying the Bible is that you keep this main thing, the main thing!

The Bible Has the Power to Change Your Life

One of the most exciting things about being a pastor is that I get to see firsthand how people's lives are changed by God's Word, the Bible. I have seen men go into prison with totally disheveled lives. They had gotten themselves into all kinds of trouble and had hurt many others along the way. But in prison they turned to the Bible. With each new visit, I could see their faith growing as they drank in the Scriptures!

There is power in God's book. By learning it, we let him restore our lives and make them new.

The Bible changes us from miserable, guilty sinners into happy, guilt-free saints! All people know deep down inside that there is something desperately wrong with their lives. We all know that we constantly fall short of the perfection God demands. Deep down we know we are accountable to God. Because of our guilt, we feel a cloud over us and sense an impending doom. Those who say they don't know this are just suppressing their knowledge. That's why many people stay away from conversations about God. They are scared of God, and talking about him reminds them of their guilt.

But what all people do not know naturally is that God loves them so much that he sent his own Son to pay for their sins and take away their guilt. You only learn that message in the Bible, but once you get it, wow! The change that takes place! I have seen people depressed and gloomy over what they have done learn what the Bible says and, in literally minutes, become lighthearted and free—simply by hearing and believing the good news of Jesus! I suspect that the Bible has already had this dramatic effect on your life.

The Bible also has the power to help us discern our own hearts and learn how to differentiate a good path from a bad one. Our hearts are deceitful and can easily lead us astray (Jeremiah 17:9). But God's Word is a light for our path through life.

When Jesus defeated the devil in the wilderness, what did he use? The Word of God. He quoted Scripture. Here was the perfect Son of God, who could have done away with the devil with a lightning bolt from his little finger, but instead he chose to be the perfect Son of Man and use Scripture in the way God had always intended. Scripture directed how he dealt with each of Satan's temptations.

But in the end, as one missionary said when people asked him how he knew whether the Bible was true or not, he told them, "Just read it." Just read it and you will see.

The Story of the Old Testament

Let's become familiar with the basic content of the Bible's history. Have you ever read CliffsNotes study guides? High school and college kids buy them all the time. They are little booklets written to summarize and simplify larger books. The students get them to review (and sometimes to avoid reading) the entire work. The booklet moves so quickly that you can hold all the thoughts together more easily. You don't lose sight of the forest by looking too closely at the trees.

The next two chapters of this book are really CliffsNotes for the Old and New Testaments. They will help you see the story of the Bible as a whole. In fact, if you reread them a few times, you will have the Bible's outline in your heart. That way, whenever you concentrate on one part of the Bible, you will know where you are in the big picture.

Before we start, let me make one other point about the content of the Bible. When my children were small, I used to love telling them stories, especially when we were cooped up in a car for a long road trip. There's nothing like a good story to shorten a drive. My favorite stories had four fictional characters, each representing one of my four sons. My boys would sit in rapt attention, listening closely to see what their own character was up to. Sometimes when I didn't quite tell the story the way one of the boys wanted, he said, "Dad, no! Don't make him do that! Instead, make him the hero." That's when I would remind them, "Hey, who's telling this story? It's my story, and I will tell it how I want to."

It is the same way with the Bible. We have to remember that when we read it, it's not our story. It's God's. The plot might not progress as I would have written it. Some stories get a much more detailed treatment than others. Even more frustrating is the fact that there are many details God has chosen to leave out—things that I am curious about. But what he does tell us is exactly what he wants us to hear, and more important, it is exactly what we need to know. The Bible is not like the history book you read in high school, where the details of history were unfolded merely for the sake of learning history. The details God has given us in his Word are there so we understand his plan of salvation.

In the pages that follow is an overview of the history of the Old Testament. It will start at the beginning of the world and move forward all the way to 430 B.C. We will cover a lot of territory. As you read, remember that the history you are reading here is his-story. It's best to approach it with an open heart and a mind that doesn't demand anything. You just want to know what God wants you to know. When you do that, you will really start to understand him.

Creation to the Tower of Babel
Genesis 1–11

"In the beginning." That's where the Bible starts. In the beginning God created human beings and everything on this earth and the vast universe around us.

In the beginning the earth was a formless mass. Over six days God gave shape to this raw form, giving it order and complexity. On the first day, God created light. On the second day, he created the expanse above the world we call the sky. On the third day, he made dry land, creating oceans and continents. Then he created plants of color and delicacy—from the smallest violet to the most massive redwood. On the fourth day, God made the sun, moon, and stars—then set them in motion, dividing days, months, and seasons. On the fifth day, he made the birds that live in the sky and the fish that live in lakes and oceans. On the sixth day, he made animals—insects, wild animals like lions, and domestic animals like sheep and cattle.

Finally, he created a man and a woman, Adam and Eve. He told them to take care of the earth and rule over it. On the seventh day, God admired what he had done. It was all very good.

God created Adam and Eve in his own image; they were perfect and holy. He gave them one command by which they could show their love for him. They could eat from all the trees of the Garden of Eden except one, the tree of the knowledge of good and evil. If they ate from that tree, they would die.

The history of this perfect world was brief. Satan tempted Adam and Eve to disobey God and eat from that forbidden tree. They listened to Satan and ate, and that one act created a barrier of sin, anger, and hostility between human beings and God. Humanity had fallen from the perfection that God had given it!

Adam and Eve tried to hide from God, but God found them—not to destroy them but to give them a promise. God promised Adam and Eve that someday a man would be born who would defeat Satan's evil.

Yet God also placed a curse on this world. The ground would be cursed with thorns and thistles, and women would have great pain in bearing children. The relationship between husbands and wives would be damaged, and all men and women would die. For the entire time that people would live on the earth, their lives would be hard and heartbreaking. But that would make Adam and Eve, and all the people to come, yearn for a better place and time when everything would be perfect again.

We'll have to move quickly now if we're going to make it through the Bible. I wanted to tell these first stories in more detail because nothing in the Bible would make sense if we didn't know about the creation, the fall, and the promise. Only now does God's promise to send a Savior make sense.

Adam and Eve had two children, Cain and Abel. Both offered sacrifices to God. Cain offered some grain; Abel offered some animals. On the surface both sacrifices seemed good. But God only accepted Abel's sacrifice. Why?

You see, Abel believed God's promise of a Savior. He offered something to God in gratitude. But with Cain's sacrifice there was no faith and, therefore, no gratitude. Because he was jealous of Abel, Cain killed him. It's a story we'll hear again and again. Friction between those who believe God's promise and those who don't is an underlying theme of Bible history. Abel had chosen the path that leads to eternal life through God's promise. Cain had chosen the path that leads to eternal death.

In the years that followed, most people lost sight of God's promise. So God sent a flood to destroy the world. It was a big flood, a very big flood. Rains covered the whole world and destroyed every living thing.

To preserve his promise, however, God chose one man and his family and told them to build a ship called an ark. When the ark was finished, God sent him passengers—animals of every kind. When the waters finally disappeared, the world had a fresh start. God gave the people a simple command: Spread out, and fill the world.

But instead, they built a city with a tower as a monument to what people could accomplish. God put a stop to this. He confused people's languages so they couldn't work together. Their tower came to be called the Tower of Babel. *Babel* means confusion.

Then he sent the people away in groups. From these groups came the great civilizations of the world.

The Patriarchs
Genesis 12–50

A tremendous amount of time is packed into the first 11 chapters of Genesis. We're only 11 chapters into the Bible, but we have covered nearly half the world's history.

To keep his promise to send a Savior from being forgotten, God chose one man to be the father of a new and great nation. The man's name was Abraham. God wanted Abraham to pass on his promise to his descendants to keep it from being forgotten and to live in the hope the promise gave.

Beginning with chapter 12 in Genesis, the Bible stops telling general world history and restricts its focus to one family, the family of Abraham. The rest of the groups of people in the world get mentioned only as their paths cross with the family of Abraham.

God led Abraham to a land called Canaan. God promised to give that land to Abraham's family.

God also promised Abraham that he and his wife, Sarah, would have a son. This was a remarkable promise because Abraham was 75 years old and Sarah was 65. What's more, God made them wait 25 more years before he fulfilled that promise. As you can imagine, Abraham struggled to hold on to God's promise. Abraham and Sarah went back and forth as they struggled to set aside their human common sense and believe God's promise. Once they even devised a plan to have a son with their servant girl, Hagar. They thought that "legally" Hagar's son could be the son God had promised. It was a futile attempt to help God accomplish his will. The result was the birth of the entire Arabian race. But God had promised that Abraham and Sarah would have a son, not Abraham and Hagar. Abraham continued clinging to that promise and waiting for God to give him a son. Finally, in her old age, Sarah bore Abraham their first child, Isaac.

Isaac is the second of the patriarchs, as they are called. When Isaac was in his 40s, his wife, Rebekah, bore him twin sons, Esau and Jacob.

What a story their family life is! It is filled with intrigue and trickery, with plots and double crosses. It is a story of struggle between brothers, much like the struggle between Cain and Abel but with a better ending.

Above all, it is the story of God's passing on his promise by choosing Jacob and his descendants as the people through whom the Savior would be born. God tested Jacob, blessed Jacob, and disciplined Jacob just as he had his father and grandfather. God gave Jacob 12 sons. Two have very important roles in Bible history.

The Savior would come through descendants of Jacob's fourth son, Judah. And Jacob's 11th son, Joseph, would save the world from famine.

Even if you don't know a lot about the Bible, you may know of Joseph's coat of many colors. The coat was a special gift from his father, Jacob. The coat also inspired treachery. When Joseph's brothers saw that Jacob favored Joseph, they hated Joseph. One day some of his brothers decided to kill him. But his brothers Reuben and Judah intervened; instead, the brothers sold Joseph to some traveling slave traders.

Joseph was taken to Egypt where he was sold to Potiphar, a high ranking official who served the king of Egypt, the pharaoh. In Potiphar's house Joseph became the highest ranking servant.

Potiphar's wife lusted after Joseph and tried to seduce him. He resisted, and she accused Joseph of rape. Potiphar became angry and threw Joseph into prison.

Even though this was one of the darkest periods in Joseph's life, God was with him and was working out a magnificent plan. In prison Joseph met two of Pharaoh's officials, who had also been accused of crimes. One night those imprisoned officials had dreams. Joseph interpreted their dreams and his interpretations came true. One of the men was executed. The other man was reinstated into service in Pharaoh's palace. Still, for two more years Joseph sat in prison.

Then the pharaoh himself had a wild and troubling dream. None of Pharaoh's trusted advisors could interpret it. Finally, the reinstated official who had been imprisoned with Joseph remembered that Joseph had interpreted his dream. He told Pharaoh about him, and Pharaoh sent for Joseph.

Joseph interpreted Pharaoh's dream. "Seven years of rich harvests will be followed by seven years of famine. Don't waste the food from the good years. Save, or Egypt and the rest of the world will starve." Through Joseph, God was saving his people so that his promise to send a Savior from their lineage would be preserved. If the world's population had died of starvation, Jacob and his family would have died and God could not have fulfilled his promise.

This is where God's magnificent plan for Joseph began to bloom. Pharaoh wondered who could manage Egypt's food storage program. He decided that it had to be Joseph.

Back in Canaan, Jacob and his sons, Joseph's brothers, were hungry. Their families were beginning to starve. Along with the rest of the world, they looked for help in Egypt—from Joseph, the brother they had sold into slavery. But they didn't recognize him.

At first Joseph hid his identity from his brothers. He devised a plan where he would lead them to repent of their sin and then give them honor and prosperity. This is a great testimony to Joseph's wisdom and love.

After Joseph revealed himself to his brothers, he invited them, along with their father, Jacob, to live in Egypt.

Genesis ends with the deaths of Jacob and Joseph. Before he died, Joseph made his brothers swear to bring his bones back to Canaan. Joseph knew God's promise to Abraham would come true. Someday his people would be given the land of Canaan as God had promised. As a great man of faith and a good teacher, he made sure that each succeeding generation would hear God's promise repeated as they learned why they were saving his bones.

Freedom and Conquest
Exodus to Joshua

Here's where the Lord puts a huge gap in his-story. More than three hundred years went by between the first and second book of the Bible. We are told nothing about the history of God's people during that time. We just know that they were in Egypt. But remember, it's God's story and he can tell it as he wants to.

The Israelites enjoyed good years in Egypt at first, growing into a large nation. But an evil pharaoh made the people of Israel into a slave nation, even killing off their baby boys to control the population. Yet, as usual, God worked behind the scenes, preparing one man to deliver God's people from Egypt. The man's name was Moses.

God blessed the daring plan of Moses' mother to save her son from death at Pharaoh's hands. Miraculously, Moses was adopted by Pharaoh's daughter.

For 40 years Moses grew up as the son of Pharaoh's daughter. Yet Moses knew he was an Israelite. He could not watch his people be mistreated. One day he defended an Israelite who was being beaten by an Egyptian. Moses killed the Egyptian.

Moses fled Egypt for fear of losing his life. He went to a land called Midian and became a shepherd. For 40 years he lived quietly in the desert. There God trained him in the ways of desert life. Finally, when Moses was ready, God called him to lead the Israelites out of Egypt and into Canaan. Moses was 80 years old.

God sent Moses to Pharaoh with the command, "Let my people go" (Exodus 5:1). Pharaoh refused, so God sent plagues on Egypt to force Pharaoh to let the Israelites go. Pharaoh would not bend. There were ten plagues in all. In the last plague, God sent the angel of death to put to death the firstborn in every Egyptian family. That was the last straw. That night Pharaoh drove the Israelites from his land.

The people of Israel went south, seemingly panic-stricken and confused. Pharaoh changed his mind again and pursued them, pinning them against the Red Sea. But God cleared a path for the Israelites through the middle of the sea. When the Egyptians followed, God brought the waters over them. In one stroke God saved the people through whom he would fulfill his promise and destroyed their enemies. No one would destroy this people until the Savior was born from their family tree!

The Israelites headed further south to Mount Sinai. There God made a formal agreement, a covenant, with the Israelites, setting them aside as his own special people. God told them to prepare themselves because he was going to show himself to them in a powerful way. God came down on Mount Sinai in fire, smoke, and thunder. He gave them the Ten Commandments and many other laws with which they governed their nation. He fleshed out his will for every aspect of their lives.

He reminded the Israelites of all the wonderful things he had done for them. "I carried you on eagles' wings," he told them, "and brought you to myself"(Exodus 19:4). Then he gave the Israelites the terms of his covenant: He would bless them and make them into a great and influential nation, if only they would obey him. They all said, "Yes, we agree to that."

The truth is that the laws were so detailed that none of the Israelites could keep them. They all had to admit that they were sinners. They lived their whole lives being shown that they needed God's forgiveness. Even though there were many laws that condemned them, embedded within those laws were pictures of the promised Savior. For example, the people were to offer many animal sacrifices, such as the Passover lamb, to teach them that sin was serious. Animals were put to death in place of sinful people, pointing them to the coming Savior.

God also had his people build a tent where he lived among them. There they could worship him and find forgiveness for their sins.

After a few weeks, God told his people that it was time to go north and take the land of Canaan. The people refused to take Canaan because they were afraid of the people in the land. God became angry with their lack of faith and made them live in the desert for another 40 years, until all the adults that had left Egypt had died. The only two men, from among those original adults, who would see the Promised Land were Joshua and Caleb.

Finally, after 40 years, God led the Israelites north onto the plains of Moab opposite the city of Jericho. Then they were poised to take the land. Moses gave the Israelites final instructions before they entered the Promised Land. He recorded these instructions in the book of the Bible called Deuteronomy.

The Israelites stood ready to cross the Jordan River and take the land of Canaan. Moses had turned over leadership to Joshua. The story of how God enabled Joshua to take the land is recorded in the book that bears his name, Joshua.

God finally fulfilled his promise to Abraham to give him the land of Canaan. But would the Israelites remain faithful to their gracious God? That's the sad part of the story.

Judges and Kings
Judges to 2 Samuel (1 Chronicles)

After Joshua's death, the Israelites began mingling with the people of the land, marrying their daughters, and joining them as they worshiped their false gods. For the next several hundred years, the Israelites were on a roller coaster. They broke God's covenant, and God let their enemies take over portions of their land. They would cry out to God, "Deliver us." God would provide a leader to deliver them. But then they would fall back into their old ways. That terrible cycle repeated itself again and again.

The rulers God sent during that period were some of the most colorful and interesting people in the Bible—judges, as they are often called. There was left-handed Ehud, who defeated Eglon, the obese king of Moab; Deborah, whose wisdom and courage gave the Israelites the resolve to fight the Canaanites; Gideon, who defeated thousands of Midianites with only three hundred Israelites but later succumbed to vanity; Samson, the man of legendary strength who helped the Israelites fight against the Philistines but was often tempted by lust; Jepthah, who sacrificed his own daughter. The judges were only dimly lit stars in the dark night of Israel's unbelief. Most Israelites had lost sight of God's promise and had turned from God's laws.

God's plan to make Israel a light shining in a dark world was not succeeding. Only a few people—like Ruth, Naomi, and Boaz, whose lives and faith we hear about in the book of Ruth—still remained faithful to God's promise of a Savior. At the end of this time, God gave the Israelites one final judge—in some ways the greatest of them all. His name was Samuel.

Samuel's mother, Hannah, hadn't been able to have children, so she promised God that if he gave her a child, she would dedicate that child for service in God's portable temple, the tabernacle. God answered her prayer.

Hannah brought her young child to the tabernacle and placed him under the care of the priest Eli. As the years passed, it became clear that God would use this boy in a special way. Under Samuel's leadership, the Israelites drove the Philistines from the land, something even Samson had not done.

But something was brewing in Israel. For more than three hundred years, Israel had no constant leader. Millions of people lived in a country with no one in charge, or so it seemed. Yet God was in charge. "Even though you cannot see me," he said, "trust that I will lead you wisely and bless you." But the Israelites didn't trust God enough to be comfortable with his plan.

They sent leaders to confront Samuel, saying, "Give us a king, someone we can see, like the other nations have." Reluctantly, Samuel agreed, but not before warning the people that having a king wouldn't be the bed of roses they expected.

God appointed Saul, a man of remarkable physical ability, to be the first king. At first Saul acted humbly and served well, but in time he became proud and turned from God's ways. Even while Saul was king, God chose Saul's successor. That was David, the greatest of all of Israel's kings and one of the most important figures of the Bible.

After Saul's death, David took the throne of Israel. God blessed David and gave him military victories, making Israel a great world power. David made the city of Jerusalem his capital and made plans for a great temple where people from all over the land would come to worship God.

What made David so important was his relationship to God's promise. God told David that he would establish David's throne forever and that one of David's sons would be the Messiah, the future King and Savior of the world.

David may have been a great king, but he was still a sinful human being. On one occasion David sank deeply into sin. He committed adultery with the beautiful wife of one of his soldiers, and when she became pregnant, he had her husband killed in battle to cover it up. It was the darkest period of David's life. Yet God had mercy on him and called him back to faith. When he had returned to God, he wrote Psalm 51. It is a beautiful psalm for anyone who is feeling the weight of his or her sins.

Much of 2 Samuel records the trouble God sent into David's life to make it clear to David and to everyone else that God did not condone what David had done. It tells how David's own son Absalom launched a military coup against his own father and drove him from Jerusalem. It tells of God's mercy on David, how God put down Absalom's rebellion and restored a humble David to his throne in Jerusalem.

The Divided Kingdom
1,2 Kings (2 Chronicles)

David's son Solomon followed him as king in Jerusalem. In Solomon we see a man of great achievements and also great failures. When Solomon was only 20 years old, God came to him in a dream and offered him anything he wanted. Solomon asked for wisdom to guide God's people. God gave him wisdom along with unimaginable wealth and honor too.

In spite of his wisdom, however, Solomon did many foolish and sinful things. Solomon married many wives, the daughters of the kings of the surrounding nations. These women brought their idols into Solomon's palace, and he worshiped them. Also, he engaged in great building projects, sapping Israel's resources.

Yet Solomon, like David, was in some ways a picture of the promised Savior. He built a great temple in Jerusalem to replace the tabernacle that the Israelites had built at Mount Sinai. The name *Solomon* means "peace," which is what his reign brought to Israel and what the Savior would bring to the world.

But Solomon's building projects took a heavy toll on the common people of Israel—a toll so great that the northern part of the nation was ready to break away if Solomon's son acted like his father.

When Solomon died, northern ambassadors asked Solomon's son Rehoboam, "Are you going to lower taxes and ease our burden or keep doing what your father did?" Rehoboam didn't see the seriousness of the situation. He answered, "If you think my father, Solomon, was bad, you haven't seen anything yet." Foolish pride, bad judgment. The ten northern tribes then broke free from Rehoboam's leadership.

The nation of Israel was permanently split in two. The northern tribes kept the name Israel. The southern two tribes took the name Judah. Things get complicated at this point, with two sets of kings. The books of 1 and 2 Kings and 2 Chronicles record the lives and times of the kings of Israel and Judah. In recording this history, the writers go back and forth between the Northern and Southern Kingdoms.

Let's start in the north, in Israel. The kingdom of Israel lasted about two hundred years. During those two hundred years, nine families, or dynasties, ruled. Six of the nineteen kings were assassinated. Two kings were overthrown by military takeovers. To the very last one, Israel's kings were wicked men who did not serve the Lord.

The first king of Israel was Jeroboam. He led the people of Israel when they split away from Judah. Jeroboam set the pace for the history of Israel. To keep his subjects from going into the Southern Kingdom to worship at Jerusalem, he set up alternate places of worship in Israel. At this point idolatry began to take over the land.

Another king named Ahab, along with his wife, Jezebel, firmly established Canaanite Baal worship in Israel and killed most of God's prophets. Two great prophets of that time, Elijah and Elisha, stood courageously against these evils, but they could not reform the nation.

Behind the scenes, God had been creating a world power, the kingdom of Assyria, to carry out his judgment against the Northern Kingdom. In 722 B.C., Samaria, the capital of the Northern Kingdom, fell to the Assyrians. To break their national pride, the Assyrians transported the people of Israel to other places in their empire. We never hear of the Northern Kingdom again.

Now let's look at what happened in the Southern Kingdom of Judah. Solomon's son Rehoboam managed to hold on to the southern tribes of Judah and Benjamin. Many of Judah's kings remained faithful to the Lord and under their leadership God's people continued to worship him at the temple in Jerusalem.

While the Assyrians were capturing the Northern Kingdom, Hezekiah, a faithful, God-fearing king, ruled over the Southern Kingdom of Judah. Through Hezekiah's God-pleasing leadership, God spared Jerusalem and allowed the nation of Judah to have eight more kings and live on for another 130 years.

Yet Judah's days also were numbered. Judah should have learned from God's punishment on the people of the Northern Kingdom, but it didn't. In fact, Judah became even more wicked than Israel had been. So God prepared another nation to punish Judah, the nation of Babylon.

Captivity and Release
Ezra to Esther, Daniel

The new superpower in the region was the nation of Babylon, located southeast of Assyria. Babylon conquered Assyria and then conquered the nations of the Assyrian Empire. This brought Babylon to the doorstep of Jerusalem.

Because the people of Judah had rejected God, he withdrew his protection from the city of Jerusalem. The city fell to the Babylonian army, which destroyed the city, including the temple Solomon had built. The Babylonians plundered all of Judah's treasures, including the ark of the covenant, and took its people into captivity.

The Babylonians used the same tactics for destroying national pride that the Assyrians had used. They took the people of Judah out of the land and settled them far away. The Jews wept as they left their beloved land and trudged off in humility as slaves of a nation that did not know the true God. "We will return soon," they thought. "God will come to our rescue. He has in the past. We can count on him now." Yes, they could count on him, but God was not willing to act according to their timetable. Jeremiah had foretold that the Jews would live in Babylon for 70 years. God sent a prophet named Ezekiel into captivity with the people. Ezekiel told them to settle down and await the Lord's deliverance.

During their 70-year stay in Babylon, the Lord kept close watch over his remnant people. He raised up the prophet Daniel, who became a great statesman, serving under all the kings of Babylon. Whenever the kings of Babylon became proud of their accomplishments and military might, God would cause something to happen to them and then lead Daniel to help them understand the meaning of the event. Daniel would say something to the effect: "You may have captured God's people, but that's only because God wanted you to. Don't become proud. God is in control of Babylon and every other nation on earth."

One time Daniel's enemies got him thrown into a lions' den. But God made the lions tame and kept Daniel alive. This miracle prompted the pagan king to issue a decree: "In every part of my kingdom people must fear and reverence the God of Daniel. For he is the living God and he endures forever; his kingdom will not be destroyed, his dominion will never end"(Daniel 6:26).

In time God raised up another world empire, the Persians. The 70 years of captivity had passed. God's time to deliver his people had come. God led one of Persia's first kings, Cyrus, to decree that the Israelites could return to their homeland and rebuild their city and their temple. By this time they were most often called Jews, after the tribe of Judah.

Seventy years after they had left for Babylon, a small but dedicated group of Jewish people returned to their homeland. Under the leadership of a king named Zerubbabel and a high priest named Joshua, the people rebuilt the temple in Jerusalem. It took them almost 20 years.

Sometime later God sent two more Jewish men from Persia to Israel to help the people rebuild the walls of Jerusalem. These were the priest and scribe Ezra and a believing court official named Nehemiah.

God cared for his people throughout those years, keeping faith alive in the hearts of his people that someday God would send them a Savior. He even protected them from a sinister plot of a Persian official to wipe them out on a single day. You can read about it in the book of Esther.

The history of God's people in their homeland during the next four hundred years is not recorded in Scripture. Yet God continued to work through the leaders of world governments, allowing them to do only what he wanted.

This is where the history of the Old Testament ends.

Books of Wisdom
Job to Song of Songs

In the middle of the Old Testament, you will find five books of wisdom. They were written at various times throughout the history of Israel. They are grouped together because they were all written in Hebrew poetic forms and focus on wisdom for life rather than history. In these books God gave the Israelites wisdom for living as his people, prayers they could use, and songs to sing when they worshiped him.

The first of these five special books is Job. Job was not an Israelite. He may have been a contemporary of Abraham. He lived in the years after the Tower of Babel, when most people had abandoned the faith. But Job was an exception to this. He worshiped the true God. Yet God sent suffering into Job's life. You'll have to read the book to find out why. Job teaches us that we can trust that God always loves us even when every earthly thing in our lives makes it look otherwise. One of the most beautiful prophecies about the coming Savior is found in Job 19:23-27. Job's ordeal made him a stronger believer, and his story has helped countless other believers endure suffering and not abandon their faith.

The second of the five books is Psalms. Psalms are hymns that can be used either as prayers or as songs. About half the psalms were written by David. Various other believers wrote the rest. Many were composed by the men who served at the temple in Jerusalem.

The Psalms has enriched the lives of God's people for thousands of years. Many use the psalms as prayers to God—expressing their joys, sorrows, and even their frustrations. Especially comforting are the psalms in which the writer pours out his heart to God in repentance over sin and expresses his comfort in God's forgiveness. There is a wide range of emotions expressed in Psalms. The psalms also vary widely in their messages. As believers become familiar with them, they find favorite psalms that they return to again and again. Many churches use the psalms in worship services. They set the pace for worship today just as they did for God's Old Testament people.

Some have called the psalms the prayers of the Messiah, the Savior. It's as though the psalm writer was led into the future and prayed in words Jesus would use. For example, Psalm 22:1 expresses Jesus' words from the cross: "My God, my God, why have you forsaken me?" In Psalm 69:21 we find these words: "They put gall in my food and gave me vinegar for my thirst." These words are clearly referring to the wine vinegar the soldiers gave Jesus to drink when he said, "I am thirsty" (John 19:28). In Psalm 16:10 Jesus rejoices that God raised him from the dead: "You will not abandon me to the grave, nor will you let your Holy One see decay." Because of its prophecies about Jesus, it is the Old Testament book that is most often quoted in the New Testament.

The last three wisdom books were written by David's son Solomon. Remember, Solomon was the wisest man who ever lived.

The book of Proverbs is a collection of sayings. In Proverbs, Solomon gives believers insights into life and instructions on how to live wisely in service to God. The proverbs deal with issues that range from the use of money to whom one should marry to the qualities of a God-fearing woman. Some Proverbs are very general and apply to every part of Christian life. For example, "Trust in the LORD with all your heart and lean not on your own understanding; in all your ways acknowledge him, and he will make your paths straight" (Proverbs 3:5,6). Other proverbs give more specific instruction. For example, "Pride only breeds quarrels, but wisdom is found in those who take advice" (Proverbs 13:10).

The fourth of the five special books is named Ecclesiastes. *Ecclesiastes* means "the preacher." The preacher, of course, is Solomon.

Solomon tried to discover how to live so that life has lasting value. Solomon approached his question not so much in terms of eternal life, but in terms of life in this present world. Can a person find meaning through riches or building projects or acquiring wisdom and knowledge? Does fame give true meaning to a person's life?

Solomon had the ability and the money to try everything in his search for meaning. And he did try everything. He indulged his every ambition and explored every source of pleasure this world can offer. When he was done, he shared his discoveries in Ecclesiastes.

The fifth of these special books is the Song of Songs, or Song of Solomon. The Song of Songs depicts the love between a man and a woman. The ancient Israelites would not let their children read this book until they were 30 years old. When you read it, you will understand why. The two lovers have imaginative and amorous descriptions of one another. This book pictures God's love for his church. It is also a wonderful display of the beautiful love God created for husbands and wives to share.

The Prophets
Isaiah to Malachi

The last 17 books of the Old Testament were written by prophets. To understand why these books are in the Bible, we must understand how important the prophets were to God's people, the Israelites.

God had delivered the people of Israel from captivity in Egypt, making them his own people and giving them a wonderful land in which to live. If only they had remained faithful to him, how wonderful their future would have been—continual prosperity, no disease, abundant rainfall, and never a worry about attacks from hostile nations.

As we have seen, the Israelites did not follow God's path. They rejected God. Although they did not realize it, their future was bleak. If they continued worshiping idols, God would take away their freedom and finally their land. Worst of all, those who did not repent of their sins would suffer eternity apart from God.

That is where the prophets came in. God wanted the Israelites to repent. So he sent men to awaken them. We have already met Elijah and Elisha.

Elijah and Elisha did not write books of the Bible. God led many of the prophets, however, to write down their prophecies. The Bible organizes their books into two groups. Five books, Isaiah through Daniel, form the first group. The last 12 begin with Hosea and end with Malachi. Each group is roughly organized by time, the earlier prophets coming first. The prophets worked for about four hundred years. Some worked primarily in the Northern Kingdom of Israel; some worked primarily in the Southern Kingdom of Judah.

Obadiah and Joel were among the earliest prophets. They prophesied in Judah. Joel pictured God's coming judgment as a locust plague—the invading armies scaling the walls of Jerusalem and working their way into every house.

Somewhat later, Amos and Hosea worked in Israel, foretelling its impending doom. About that time God sent a prophet by the name of Jonah. He was called to preach to the unbelieving people of Ninevah, the capital of Assyria, which was soon to be Israel's archenemy. Jonah resisted God's command because he hated the Assyrians. He fled by ship in the opposite direction from Assyria. God sent a storm that almost shipwrecked the boat, yet to save Jonah, he caused Jonah to be swallowed by a huge fish. After Jonah repented of his hardened heart, God caused the fish to regurgitate him on the shoreline at the east end of the Mediterranean Sea, in effect pointing Jonah toward Nineveh. Then Jonah went to Nineveh and succeeded in his mission to bring the people to faith. Through Jonah, the Lord saved many people and kept the Assyrians in power so that they could be his servants to punish the Northern Kingdom of Israel.

Later, when Assyria was threatening the Northern Kingdom of Israel, God sent the prophets Isaiah and Micah. Isaiah deserves special mention. The last part of Isaiah's book, chapters 40–66, is filled with pictures of God's power and love and with prophecies about the coming Savior. In chapter 53:5 he reaches the pinnacle of messianic prophecy. He says, "He was pierced for our transgressions, he was crushed for our iniquities; the punishment that brought us peace was upon him, and by his wounds we are healed." Such prophecies are found in nearly all of the prophets. While they mostly warned about impending judgment, they also foretold the coming of the Savior and the new kingdom he would establish that would never pass away. Often their prophecies were very specific. Micah, for example, foretold that Jesus would be born in Bethlehem.

The prophet Nahum wrote to the Assyrians, telling them that they had become proud and gone too far in their acts of cruelty and that God would punish them for their ruthless treatment of Israel.

After the Northern Kingdom was gone, God sent the prophets Zephaniah and Habakkuk to Judah to warn about God's impending judgment. He also sent Jeremiah, one of the greatest of the prophets. But the people would not listen to him either. Jeremiah told about the new covenant in Jesus' blood that would replace the old covenant based on the law.

After the people of Judah had been taken captive into Babylon, God sent Ezekiel and Daniel to urge them to accept God's discipline and look forward to God's deliverance.

When God finally delivered the people of Judah and allowed them to return to their homeland, he commissioned them to rebuild his temple. When the project was not getting done, he sent Haggai and Zechariah to encourage the people to rebuild the temple and repair the fallen walls of Jerusalem.

One hundred years later, God sent a final prophet, Malachi, who prophesied about the great forerunner of the Messiah and the coming Savior himself. After Malachi's death, God did not send any more prophets. He chose to remain silent for more than four hundred years.

If this were our story, we would add information that talks about the 400-plus years between the last book of the Old Testament and the first book of the New Testament. Much information about this period can be learned from other sources, but as we said in the beginning, this is not our story. It is God's. And by his grace we know all that we need to know.

We know that in the beginning God made all people to be perfect and holy. We know that Adam and Eve sinned shortly after they were made. We know that every one of their descendants is born a sinner just like them. We know that right after they sinned, God promised to send a Savior to take away sin and death. We know that throughout Old Testament history, God promised over and over again to send that Savior. With each new prophecy, God added more detail about the Savior's life and purpose.

We also know that God chose a certain people from the family of Abraham to be his own special people. They lived under the promise that God gave to Abraham. They also lived as a people set apart from the world under a temporary covenant, the law covenant God gave them through Moses. They would live under God's laws and his promises until, from their own lineage, the Savior would be born.

That is really all we need to know. It is God's story, and we need to hear it! Now that you have read this overview of the Old Testament, you are ready to embark on a similar journey through the New Testament. As you do, remember it will still be His-story! Look for the details he wants you to remember. And enjoy yourself. You are getting to know the greatest story ever told. By the way, have you noticed that swimming in the Bible is becoming easier?

THE STORY OF THE NEW TESTAMENT

Introduction

In many ways you cannot understand events in history unless you know the settings for those events. So as I begin telling you New Testament history, I want to set the scene by going through a little of the history between the last book of the Old Testament and the first book of the New. When Old Testament times ended more than four hundred years earlier, God's people, the Jews, had been allowed to return from captivity in Babylon and were nestled back in their homeland. Their temple had been rebuilt, and the faithful were waiting for the promised Savior.

Under Persian rule, the Israelites were allowed a lot of freedom. But still they were a very small player in world politics. Israel's independence under Persian rule came to an end when Alexander the Great, the young and ambitious king of Greece, defeated Persia in 333 B.C. and established Greek rule throughout the world. From that time on, warring ethnic groups battled over that little strip of land between the Mediterranean Sea and the Jordan River, which we call the Holy Land. The high points of this history are symbolized in the last chapters of the book of Daniel. They are also told in detail in ancient books called the books of the Maccabees, which are not included in our Scriptures. In 63 B.C. the new world power, mighty Rome, conquered the Holy Land. Rome would rule the Jews for hundreds of years. The Jews had a deep yearning to be free and looked forward to "David's Son," who, they believed, would free them from Rome.

The most common language in the world at this time was Greek, and most people learned to speak some Greek even if they had a different first language. Greek was a lot like English is today.

There were trade routes running through the Holy Land, so although Israel was small, there were always a good number of world travelers spending time there. The Roman occupation and the trade routes forced the Jews to deal with Gentiles on a daily basis.

47

Also, for many centuries Jews had been dispersed throughout the Mediterranean basin. When Jesus was born, there aleady were Jewish synagogues in Rome, Asia Minor, northern Africa, and Greece. All of these Jews had learned different languages growing up, but their one common denominator was their faith and their love for the temple in Jerusalem. They would try to get to Jerusalem for the three great feasts as often as they could, especially for the Passover festival in the spring.

During this era the everyday Jewish faith of the people changed dramatically from what it had been in Old Testament times. Simple adherence to Moses' laws gave way to religious sects. Traditionalists joined the sect of the Pharisees, who established many rules for daily living that they thought would make God happy. The Pharisees added hundreds of their own traditions to Moses' laws, and the whole religious system became a source of spiritual oppression for the common people.

The more liberal-minded Jews, mostly from the aristocracy, joined the Sadducees. Sadducees depended on reason more than the Word of God. They didn't believe in angels, miracles, the resurrection of the body, or heaven. Some say that is why they were Sad—you see! The Sadducees also made up most of the ruling council, called the Sanhedrin. At the head of the Sanhedrin was the high priest. By this time the office of high priest was filled not by birth but through politics and intrigue.

Right-wing militants joined the Zealots, as they were called. These Zealots were always scheming on how to overthrow Roman rule and establish an independent Israel.

Men with political savvy joined the Herodians. They were friends and associates of the various Herods ruling in the region.

Among the people was a yearning for freedom—freedom from Rome, from oppression, from poverty, and all the other social ills of the time. Yet in the hearts of those who understood the true meaning of God's Word, God kept alive a yearning for a spiritual King who would establish a kingdom in which people would be at peace with God. God had not forgotten his people, or his promise.

Jesus' Early Years

Amid the roar of the political struggles and religious wrangling of the day, God broke his four hundred years of silence. Yet the Lord broke it only with a whisper. He broke it by sending an angel to a priest named Zechariah, telling him that he and his wife, Elizabeth, would have a son who would be a great prophet and prepare the way for the greatest prophet of all.

About six months later, an angel came to a young woman named Mary and told her she would have a child. He would be the Savior of the world. Immediately Mary visited her cousin Elizabeth. Elizabeth was six months along in her pregnancy. Mary said to Elizabeth, "[God] has helped his servant Israel, remembering to be merciful to Abraham and his descendants forever, even as he said to our fathers" (Luke 1:54,55).

When Zechariah's son was born, Zechariah said, "You, my child, will be called a prophet of the Most High; for you will go on before the Lord to prepare the way for him, to give his people the knowledge of salvation through the forgiveness of their sins" (Luke 1:76,77). Zechariah's son was named John. Later he would be known as John the Baptist. He was to prepare the people for the Savior's coming. The Old Testament prophets Isaiah and Malachi had foretold his ministry.

Mary and Joseph were required to take part in a census of the entire Roman Empire. Everyone was required to go to the place of his ancestor's birth. When Mary and Joseph arrived in the town of Bethlehem, the same town where the great King David had been born, the inn was full. The couple had to find temporary shelter wherever they could. All they could find was a stable. And that's where the Savior of the world was born.

God's whisper of the Savior's arrival was broken again by a large group of angels who loudly announced the Savior's birth to a group of shepherds out in a lonely field.

Later Mary and Joseph took their son to the temple in Jerusalem to offer sacrifices for Mary's purification, which was one of the commands found in the Old Testament law. An old man came up to them, took the child in his arms, and said, "My eyes have seen your salvation, which you have prepared in the sight of all people, a light for revelation to the Gentiles and for glory to your people Israel" (Luke 2:30-32).

Some months later a group of wise scholars, called Magi, arrived in Jerusalem looking for the king of the Jews. God was leading them to worship the Messiah. Guided by a star as well as the ancient prophecy from Micah 5:2 about the Messiah being born in Bethlehem, they then went there and worshiped him.

When the ruler of Israel, King Herod, heard of this, he became jealous and tried to destroy Jesus by killing all the baby boys in Bethlehem. God warned Mary and Joseph and told them to flee to Egypt until Herod had died. A few years later God called them back, and they then settled in the northern part of the Holy Land, in Galilee in a city called Nazareth. That's where Jesus grew up.

Angels talking to lowly men and women, mostly in private; shepherds worshiping a child in a cattle stall; an old man saying strange things in a temple; non-Jews searching for a newborn king; a jealous and crazy ruler trying to wipe out opposition—nothing that would rouse the world from its sleep. So far, only a whisper.

Jesus' Ministry

Thirty years later, God's whisper about the Savior suddenly turned to a shout. God led Zechariah's son, John, into the desert around the Jordan River. "The promised Savior will soon appear. Repent!" he told the people. "Come, I will baptize you. Have your sins washed away in the Jordan River. If you do this, when the Savior comes, you will be ready to receive him and listen to what he has to say." Thousands of people went out to the Jordan River to hear John. Many were baptized. The only people who refused to listen were the religious leaders of the day, men who knew little about repentance and even less about serving God in a willing spirit.

God's silence had ended.

A short time later, Jesus came to the Jordan to be baptized by John. John saw him and cried out, "Look, the Lamb of God, who takes away the sin of the world!" (John 1:29). At Jesus' baptism, God the

Father thundered from heaven, "This is my Son, whom I love; with him I am well pleased" (Matthew 3:17). The Holy Spirit descended from heaven like a dove and landed on Jesus.

Immediately after his baptism, the Holy Spirit led Jesus out into the desert, where he did not eat or drink for 40 days. There the devil tempted him. "I will help you fulfill your mission. Do it my way," said Satan. "God is not loving enough to care for you properly." That's just what Satan had said to Adam and Eve in the Garden of Eden. But unlike Adam and Eve, Jesus did not give in to Satan's temptation. Remember God's promise that he would send a Savior to undo what Satan had done to the world through Adam and Eve? That's what Jesus was doing out in the desert. He was representing the whole world and obeying God's will. His obedience has made it possible for the sons and daughters of Adam and Eve, you and me, to stand before God and be declared innocent.

When his work in the desert was over, Jesus burst onto the public scene. Jesus' two biggest obstacles were (a) the Jews' desire for a political ruler to set them free from the power of Rome and (b) the Jews' self-righteousness that came from constantly focusing on their own good works. The masses of common folks longed for a political power, for military might, for economic prosperity, and for a new society in which hunger, disease, and religious hypocrisy would be no more. Before Jesus could win their hearts, he had to help his people understand the real nature of the kingdom he came to establish. He had to show them what John the Baptist had begun showing them—that the real tyrant was sin, not Rome; death, not political oppression.

When Jesus returned from the desert, he gathered his disciples around him. He appointed the Twelve to serve as special witnesses, or apostles. They were to watch, listen, and learn, and then once he had ascended into heaven, they were to tell the world what he had done.

What things they saw! They saw a man who did what no one had ever done before. They saw Jesus calm a violent storm, showing he had control over nature. They saw him cast out demons, showing he had power over the devil. They saw him heal hundreds of sick people, showing he had power over disease. They saw him feed thousands of people by making a little bread and fish multiply before their eyes, showing he had power over hunger. They even saw Jesus raise the dead, showing he had power over death. All this convinced them that David's long-promised descendant had finally arrived. Jesus was declared by his disciples and all who trusted in him to be the great Son of David. He was the one who would usher in God's kingdom.

And what things they heard! The people heard Jesus speak God's Word with such clarity and power that they had to confess a prophet was among them. They heard him explain God's laws as no one had ever explained them before. They heard him expose the shallowness and hypocrisy of many Jewish leaders of the day. Most important, they heard Jesus tell how he would suffer in their place for their sins. They heard him say God's Word would spread throughout the world and bring many people to repentance and faith and into his kingdom.

By what Jesus did and said, the people of his day realized he was no ordinary prophet. He was the Son of God, who would single-handedly open the door of heaven for all people through the forgiveness of their sins.

Shortly before Jesus and his disciples set out for Jerusalem to celebrate the Passover, Jesus went up on a mountain. There the Father let three of the disciples see Jesus' glory, the glory he had in heaven before he came to earth. There Moses and Elijah, two of the greatest Old Testament prophets, spoke with Jesus, the greatest prophet of all, about his impending death in Jerusalem. They talked about how he, Jesus, would save all who treasure God's promise. And they discussed how he, Jesus, would win for people a kingdom in which they would have God's love and care forever.

Jesus' Death and Resurrection

About three years after he started his ministry, Jesus rode into the city of Jerusalem on a donkey with thousands singing his praises. What must his disciples have thought when they saw this? Before this Jesus had avoided the political crowds. But now he seemed to be acting like a real king. The people threw garments and palm branches on the road to prepare his way, praising him as the Son of David. The Old Testament prophet Zechariah had prophesied that this would happened. No doubt his disciples were wondering if he finally would use his great power and authority to lead an army against Rome. That's how the most confusing week in history began.

On the next day, Jesus entered the temple courts and drove out all the moneychangers and the people who were selling sacrificial animals. In doing so he stirred hatred in the hearts of the Jewish leaders who were making money from those merchants. They schemed on how to arrest him and put him to death. Jesus spent Tuesday of his last week confronting the leaders of the Jews, the Pharisees and the Sadducees, and refuting their false teachings and hollow arguments against him.

On Thursday, Jesus told his disciples to prepare for the Passover. So far everything seemed to be going along fine, but there were signs that eroded their kingdom hopes. Jesus talked about one of them betraying him, and mysteriously Judas Iscariot left the Passover meal. Jesus washed their feet, which was hardly becoming of a king. He talked about fighting but wouldn't allow them to use swords. He said that all of them would desert him.

As was his custom, Jesus then led his disciples into the Garden of Gethsemane for prayer. Late in the evening, while Jesus prayed and the disciples slept, an armed mob approached them. Judas had conspired with the Jewish religious leaders to have Jesus arrested and killed.

The disciples were terrified. At first they wanted to fight, but Jesus would not allow them to. His kingdom could not be established by military force. That left the disciples only one option—they deserted Jesus, just as he had predicted, and fled into the night.

All alone, Jesus was arrested and led away. But you see, that's the way it had to be. Only the Son of God, who had become a human being like us, could go head-to-head with Satan and defeat him.

First Jesus was led to the high priest Caiaphas, the chief religious authority among the Jews. Many false witnesses testified against Jesus but none of them could agree. For hours Jesus stood before the court, silent, just as the prophet Isaiah had predicted. Finally, in frustration, Caiaphas stood up and commanded Jesus under oath to tell him plainly if he was the Son of God. That's when Jesus came out with it. He freely confessed that he was and that someday he would judge the world. Caiaphas tore his garment in rage. The Sanhedrin handed down the verdict. According to them Jesus was guilty of blasphemy against God. They sentenced him to death.

But the Jews needed approval from the Roman governor to carry out the death penalty. By now it was Friday morning, so they walked Jesus over to the palace of Pontius Pilate, the Roman governor of the province of Judea. Pilate wanted nothing to do with Jesus, but he buckled under pressure and sentenced Jesus to death by crucifixion. First he had him flogged. Flogging was often so brutal that people died while they were being beaten. After flogging Jesus, in a mocking gesture Pilate's soldiers twisted a crown of thorns and pressed it on his head. Then they cried, "Hail, king of the Jews!" (John 19:3). Little did they know that he was their king. He had come to die for their sins too.

Pilate's soldiers took Jesus and two others outside the city walls of Jerusalem to crucify them. When they reached *Golgotha*, which means "the place of the skull," they drove nails into Jesus' hands and feet and hoisted him up. Jesus was crucified along with two criminals.

Jesus and the other two hung on the cross Friday morning and afternoon. Most people who were crucified cursed their executioners. But instead of cursing his executioners, Jesus forgave them. He also gave instructions to his disciple John for the care of his mother. One of the criminals hanging next to Jesus repented of his sin and came to faith in Jesus. And Jesus promised him that he would be with him in heaven that very day. Everything Jesus said from the cross was filled with love. The Roman soldiers had seen dozens of crucifixions, but none like this.

At about noon the sky became black. Jesus cried out the words of one of David's psalms: "My God, my God, why have you forsaken me?" (Psalm 22:1). Looking back, we know why he said that. At that moment Jesus was carrying on himself the sins of the whole world. God had forsaken his Son so he would not have to forsake us. Finally, it was over. Jesus had fulfilled all the prophecies, and he had paid for the sins of the whole world. He said, "It is finished" (John 19:30), and gave his spirit into his Father's hands.

The greatest battle ever waged, fought on the battlefield of a Roman cross, had been won by the innocent Son of God. God had satisfied his own justice and had reconciled himself to the entire world! Now his kingdom was established, a kingdom of love based on the forgiveness of sins.

Jesus' followers removed his body from the cross and carried him to the tomb of a rich man named Joseph. That too had been prophesied by Isaiah seven hundred years earlier. It was Friday evening. Nothing extraordinary happened on Saturday, but on Sunday several of the women who had followed Jesus ran to the tomb to finish preparing his body for burial. These women were the first to hear the greatest message of all time. At the tomb they saw two angels who told them, "Jesus has risen from the dead. He is not here."

The next few weeks were filled with joy. Jesus opened his disciples' minds to understand why he died and rose. He helped them understand the real meaning of God's kingdom. It is a kingdom of grace and forgiveness, and it had finally arrived.

It is not just a kingdom for the Jews, as so many of them had hoped. Instead, it is for the whole world. The promise God had made to Adam and Eve, the promise he had reiterated to Abraham and to so many others in Old Testament history, had finally come true. God had sent a Savior for all humanity! Jesus told his disciples to go and tell everyone from every nation that he was their Savior and that someday he will come back to take his believers to be with him in heaven—a place without warfare, hunger, sorrow, death, or pain; a place where all God's people will live with him in everlasting joy into eternity.

The Early Church, Paul's First Journey
Acts 1–12, James

Forty days after Jesus rose from the dead, he went back into heaven. Before he ascended, he commissioned his apostles to go and make disciples all over the world by baptizing and by teaching everything he had taught them. In that way he would fulfill his promise to be with his people and bless their labors.

Ten days later Jesus gave the disciples the power to do the work for which he had trained them. The disciples gathered in the temple in Jerusalem along with other followers of Jesus. They were expecting something to happen, but they were not quite sure what it would be. Suddenly the Holy Spirit filled them with power and understanding. Peter and the other disciples remembered what Jesus had told them, and they began preaching with understanding and authority, just as Jesus had. That day God enabled the twelve apostles to speak in the languages of their listeners. Through this miracle, God let the early Christians know that his kingdom is for people of all languages.

Some of the people still made fun of the disciples and accused them of being drunk, so Peter stood up and preached a powerful sermon. Working from prophecies found in the Old Testament, he explained that Jesus had to suffer, die, and rise again. Peter told the Jewish people there that day that they had killed the Son of God. When they heard him, they were terrified. They cried out, "What must we do?" Peter simply replied, "Repent, and be baptized in the name of Jesus for the forgiveness of your sins. And you will receive the Holy Spirit." It is this life-giving message that the church has been proclaiming now for two thousand years.

Thousands of people came to faith that day. Jesus also gave the apostles power to perform miracles as he had. Thousands more would trust in Jesus and be baptized in the following days and weeks.

The story of the early church is filled with persecution. Peter and John, two of Jesus' closest disciples, were imprisoned and beaten. Stephen, a gifted and dedicated man, was stoned to death. Within a few years, the members of the Jerusalem church were fleeing the city in droves because of persecution. Yet the kingdom continued to grow and become stronger through the leadership of Peter and the other apostles. The church spread north into Samaria and south into the African country of Ethiopia.

While this was going on, God worked behind the scenes to prepare another leader for the church. You see, up to now the church had worked primarily among the Jewish people. God wanted someone to carry the gospel to non-Jews. The Bible calls non-Jews Gentiles. God chose an unlikely candidate: Saul, a Pharisee and an enemy of Christianity. After Stephen's death, Saul began going into Christian homes, hauling believers out, throwing them in prison, and putting them to death.

During one of Saul's trips to search out and arrest Christians, God led him to faith and set him on a course that would change the Christian church forever. For several years Paul restudied the Old Testament to learn how it had promised the coming of Jesus in so many ways. Jesus made Paul one of his special witnesses, an apostle who would join the ranks of the original twelve apostles.

There was a church on the fringe of the Christian world at that time in a city called Antioch, on the coast of the Mediterranean Sea, north of Galilee. Jews and Gentiles worshiped together in that congregation. God led the church in Antioch to send Paul and another man named Barnabas on a missionary trip to Jews and Gentiles in the areas we now know as Turkey and Greece. This was Paul's first missionary journey.

Paul's journey first took him to the island of Cyprus and then into Asia Minor, today known as Turkey. He started several congregations there. He and his fellow worker Barnabas enjoyed great success, and they suffered serious persecution. Once Paul was even stoned and left for dead, but the Lord spared his life. The gospel about Jesus gained a firm foothold in Asia Minor. Paul and Barnabas returned home to Antioch to tell the church there what great things God had done.

However, something threatened the stability of the church and jeopardized further mission work. A major question troubled many of the early Jewish Christians. Should they and the Gentiles still follow Moses' laws? The apostles, with Paul, met in Jerusalem to settle the matter. After considerable discussion, the apostles concluded that Jewish Christians were free, if they wished, to serve God by following Jewish customs, which were familiar and meaningful to them. At the same time, the church was not to insist that Gentiles follow the Jewish laws.

Paul spelled out the freedom that the gospel gives in a letter he wrote to Christians in Asia Minor. We call that letter Galatians.

As the church grew and spread, Peter began doing mission work in the surrounding areas. James, a brother of Jesus, took over the leadership of the Jerusalem church. He also wrote a book that bears his name, James.

Paul's Second Journey
Acts, 1,2 Thessalonians

Paul's next journey took him back into Asia Minor, or present-day Turkey. There Paul and his fellow worker Silas visited the churches Paul had started on his first journey. In Lystra they met Timothy, who joined the missionary team. In Troas they met Luke, a physician, who also joined them. Paul's plan was to continue doing missionary work in Asia Minor. But the Lord had another plan. One night Paul had a dream. In that dream Paul saw a man from Macedonia, the northernmost province of Greece, inviting him to come and share the gospel there.

Paul knew that the Lord, who had closed doors in Asia Minor, was opening another door to the west. It was a historic moment when Paul and his companions—Silas, Timothy, and Luke—set foot on a boat at Troas and headed out into the Aegean Sea bound for Greece. They were beginning the church's first formal mission work on the European continent.

The ship landed at Philippi. The Lord continued to lead Paul and his team—first to Lydia, who opened her heart to the gospel and her home to the missionaries. Then, while under arrest, God led Paul to a jailer who "opened" his prison to Paul and then opened his heart to the Lord.

Success for the gospel message, but persecution for the messengers—that cycle repeated itself in the days ahead.

Paul, Silas, and Timothy continued west to the city of Thessalonica. The Lord opened doors there also. Jews and Gentiles came to faith. But some Jews, jealous of Paul's success, stirred up opposition to the missionaries and forced them to leave.

Next they went to Berea. Many people came to faith, but the Jews again stirred up opposition and Paul was again forced to leave.

He departed by ship and arrived in Athens, waiting for Silas and Timothy who had stayed in Berea.

While Paul waited in Athens, he preached the gospel. He said, "Men of Athens! I see that in every way you are very religious. For as I walked around and looked carefully at your objects of worship, I even found an altar with this inscription: TO AN UNKNOWN GOD. Now what you worship as something unknown I am going to proclaim to you" (Acts 17:22,23). But sadly, when Paul mentioned the resurrection, the Athenians, given to philosophy and learning, in general tuned him out. In that city only a few people came to faith.

From Athens Paul made the short trip to Corinth and began mission work there, but Paul did not start congregations and then forget about them. His mind was troubled about what was happening in Thessalonica and the other cities to the north. Soon Timothy and Silas arrived and reported to Paul that the Thessalonians were doing well and were bearing up under persecution.

With joy in his heart, Paul wrote them a letter, which we call 1 Thessalonians. He said, "We continually remember before our God and Father your work produced by faith, your labor prompted by love, and your endurance inspired by hope in our Lord Jesus Christ. For we know, brothers loved by God, that he has chosen you, because our gospel came to you not simply with words, but also with power, with the Holy Spirit and with deep conviction" (1 Thessalonians 1:3-5).

All during his time in Corinth, Paul served the Macedonian congregations in Philippi, Thessalonica, and Berea by letter and through fellow workers such as Silas, Timothy, and Luke. Some time later Paul wrote another letter to the Thessalonians Christians, which we call 2 Thessalonians.

Getting back to Paul's work in Corinth. The Lord had many people in that city whom he would bring to faith through Paul's message. The Lord said to Paul in a dream, "Do not be afraid; keep on speaking, do not be silent. For I am with you, and no one is going to attack and harm you, because I have many people in this city" (Acts 18:9,10). So Paul stayed there for about a year and a half. Paul endured hardship during those months, but the Lord kept his enemies at bay until Paul's work there was finished.

Paul left Corinth accompanied by two Christians, Aquila and Priscilla, a husband and wife, who had become Paul's friends and coworkers. They went east across the Aegean Sea to Ephesus. Aquila and Priscilla stayed in Ephesus and Paul continued on to Jerusalem, but not without promising the Ephesian believers that he would return. Paul's promise to them points us ahead to his next missionary journey. After visiting the Christians in Jerusalem, Paul returned to his home church at Antioch.

Paul's Third Journey
Acts, 1,2 Corinthians, Romans

Paul did not remain long in Antioch. He started out across Asia Minor, visiting the churches he had begun on his first missionary journey. As promised, Paul went to Ephesus to continue his work at this important city.

Paul did not break any new ground on his third missionary journey. He worked in Ephesus for three years. Many people came to faith. Someday this city would replace Antioch as the leading city of the Christian world, just as Antioch had replaced Jerusalem.

But Ephesus was not Paul's only concern during the three years he stayed there. From sources outside the book of Acts, we learn that Paul worked hard to build up the congregation at Corinth. From Ephesus he made a trip to Corinth and wrote them at least one letter, which they answered in a letter of their own.

The Corinthian congregation was vital to Paul's missionary work. If this congregation was lost to Christ, Paul would not be able to continue his work in the west—in Rome or in Spain. God had blessed this congregation with spiritual gifts and with active leaders, but the congregation's problems were many. The list is staggering. Some of Paul's converts were looking down on his ministry. The congregation had divided into cliques, each choosing a leader who personally appealed to them. One member was committing incest, and the others were allowing it to continue, proud of their open-mindedness. Some were still worshiping idols, bad enough in itself but worse considering that worship in those days often involved going to temple prostitutes. Some were suing fellow members in court. The rich were avoiding the poor, even at worship services. They misused the Lord's Supper, treating it like a regular meal. The spiritually gifted were showing off their gifts instead of using them to help fellow members grow in faith. Worst of all, some were denying that people could rise from the dead.

Paul addressed each of these problems and more in the letter we call 1 Corinthians.

The last months of Paul's third journey were spent in Greece. When he left Ephesus, Paul hurried north to meet Titus, whom he had sent to Corinth to try to work out their problems. Paul could not rest until he heard Titus' report.

Paul finally met up with Titus in Macedonia. In general, Titus gave him a good report about the church in Corinth. But some congregation members, especially some of the leaders, were still confused about Paul's motives and his ministry. So Paul wrote them another letter, which we call 2 Corinthians. In this letter Paul poured out his heart to these Christians, describing his ministry and affirming his love for them. "I have risked everything, my very life," Paul says, "to bring you the gospel. I will not rest until I know you stand firm in Christ." Paul soon visited Corinth. We envision a reunion filled with joy and a time of productive service there.

Paul's love, however, was not restricted to the congregations he personally had started. His love went out to the whole church. He knew the believers in Jerusalem were going through difficult times. They needed financial help. Much of Paul's third missionary journey was spent gathering a collection for the needy believers in Jerusalem.

Paul enlisted the help of the Galatian congregations. The churches in Asia, around Ephesus, joined in. The churches in Macedonia, Philippi, and Thessalonica were anxious to give. After some encouragement, the Corinthians came through also. A delegation then assembled in Corinth to take the money to Jerusalem. Before he left Corinth, Paul wrote to the Christians in Rome, preparing them for his upcoming visit after he delivered the offerings to Jerusalem. They were to be his base for mission work still farther to the west. We call this letter the book of Romans, which presents the most complete statement of Christian teaching found in the Bible.

Paul and his delegation then traveled to Jerusalem through Macedonia and Asia. In Ephesus, Paul spent a few hours with the elders of the church. He said, "I have not hesitated to proclaim to you the whole will of God. Keep watch over yourselves and all the flock of which the Holy Spirit has made you overseers. Be shepherds of the church of God, which he bought with his own blood. Now I commit you to God and to the word of his grace, which can build you up and give you an inheritance among all those who are sanctified" (Acts 20:27,28,32). With this, Paul set sail for Jerusalem, not knowing what was awaiting him there.

Paul's Captivity and Trip to Rome
Acts, Ephesians, Philippians, Colossians, Philemon

For many years Paul had been free to come and go as he pleased. But the next four years would be different. Most of these years he would spend as a prisoner of the Roman state. At the end of his third missionary journey, as Paul neared Jerusalem, he stopped at Tyre where the believers warned him not to go any farther. At Caesarea the prophet Agabus predicted that Paul would be bound in Jerusalem. The people pleaded with Paul not to go. But Paul said, "Why are you weeping and breaking my heart? I am ready not only to be bound, but also to die in Jerusalem for the name of the Lord Jesus" (Acts 21:13).

The first few days he spent in Jerusalem were peaceful. Paul met with James and the other leaders. But one day some Jews saw him in the temple. Since they knew Paul associated with Gentiles, they assumed Paul had broken the law and brought a Gentile into the temple. A riot developed. The crowd seized Paul, dragged him from the temple, and tried to kill him.

The Roman commander intervened. He arrested Paul and tried to find out what crime he was guilty of. Finally, he let Paul speak to the crowd. "I am a Jew," Paul said, "I was thoroughly trained in the laws of our fathers. I grew up here in Jerusalem, sitting at the feet of the great teacher Gamaliel. I was just as serious about the law as you are. I too persecuted Christians. But here's what happened to me." Then Paul told them about how Jesus appeared to him and brought him to faith. He explained that God himself had sent him to spread the Word to the Gentiles.

When the crowd heard this, they were furious, so the Roman commander took Paul into custody. The Jews plotted to kill Paul. The Roman commander then transferred him to Caesarea, the seat of the Roman governor.

There Paul sat in prison for two years, awaiting trial. A new governor, Festus, took up his case. Paul, sensing he would not get a fair trial, demanded his right as a Roman citizen to stand trial in Rome itself.

Recall that two years earlier Paul had intended to travel to Rome and do mission work in Spain. He never thought it would be as a prisoner. But God's ways are not always our ways, are they?

Luke describes Paul's voyage to Rome in the book of Acts. What an adventure! But perhaps the ship's passengers wouldn't have called it that. The voyage is a story of a late start—too soon before winter for safe passage. It's the story of deceptively good weather that lured the ship's captain on. It's the account of a terrible storm that drove the ship for two weeks on the open sea, ending in shipwreck. Most important, it is a story of God's grace, God's care for Paul and the other passengers, and God's continued desire for Paul to spread his gospel to the Gentiles. In the middle of a storm and a shipwreck, God opened hearts to believe.

Finally Paul arrived in Rome. He awaited trial for two years under house arrest. But don't get the idea these were idle years. Paul preached the gospel at every opportunity. Representatives from his churches in Asia Minor and Greece visited him often. Men like Mark, Timothy, and Luke were there, at least some of the time, no doubt serving believers in places where Paul could not go.

Paul's pen was active during those years. He wrote a letter to Ephesus, reminding the Christians there of God's grace, explaining his own ministry to the Gentiles, and helping them live as God's people. He wrote to the Christians in Colossae, a city not far from

Ephesus, helping them see through false teachings about Christ and, in the process, giving us a letter that shows Christ in all his glory. He wrote a short letter to a man named Philemon, whose slave Onesimus had run away and come to Rome to find Paul. Paul sent Onesimus back to Philemon as a Christian and appealed to Philemon to treat Onesimus as a brother in Christ.

Paul wrote to the congregation in Philippi, thanking them for their financial help, encouraging them in the faith, and expressing confidence that he would be released and visit them soon.

This is where Luke's story of Paul's journey ends. The rest of the story we must piece together from hints in Paul's letters and from the writings of early church teachers. We will do that in the next section.

Later Years
Paul (1, 2 Timothy, Titus); Peter (1, 2 Peter); John (1-3 John, Revelation); Hebrews; Jude

When the book of Acts ends, Paul is in Rome awaiting trial. Luke may have written his gospel, Luke, and his history of the spread of Christianity, the book of Acts, sometime during the two years he waited for the Roman court to decide on Paul's fate.

Paul was released. From what we can piece together from Paul's letters and from a few scattered references in the writings of early church leaders, here's what happened.

Upon his release, Paul visited the congregations in Asia Minor and Greece. He continued to teach, to nurture, and to organize these scattered groups of believers. He knew the churches needed his ongoing care. He stationed Timothy in Ephesus to correct some problems there. He encouraged Timothy with a letter, which we call 1 Timothy. He stationed Titus on the island of Crete to appoint elders to oversee the churches. Later he wrote a letter to Titus.

Early church writers report that Paul did mission work in Spain. While Paul was in Spain, Peter may have come to Rome to help the congregations there and to oversee Paul's mission congregations during his absence. Peter wrote two letters to churches in Asia Minor. Mark worked with Peter in Rome during those later years, and some early church writers said that Mark wrote his gospel in Rome with Peter's help. Legend has it that Peter died in Rome.

Paul returned from Spain. He continued to support the churches in Asia Minor and Greece. Later in life he was arrested and sent once again to Rome to stand trial. From his last letter, a second letter to Timothy, it is clear that Paul did not expect to be released. Early church writers tell us he was martyred in Rome.

We might mention a few books we have not touched on yet. The apostle Matthew wrote a gospel, possibly the first of the four gospels. A brother of Jesus, Jude, wrote a short letter. This letter may have been written later, after Peter wrote his second letter, since it underscores much of what Peter wrote. An unknown author wrote to Jewish Christians, Hebrews as they are called, encouraging them not to give up on Jesus, no matter what persecutions they had to endure.

Late in his life, the apostle John served the church in Ephesus. He wrote the gospel that goes by his name, John, and three letters that also go by his name, 1, 2, and 3 John.

The last book of the New Testament is the book of Revelation, also written by the apostle John when he was in exile on an island called Patmos. In one of the visions Jesus gave to John, he saw a great multitude that no one could count, from every tribe and people and nation and language. Sitting on the throne was a lamb. The people around the throne called out, "Salvation belongs to our God, who sits on the throne, and to the Lamb" (Revelation 7:10). John was recording the great scene in heaven, where all the believers from the Old Testament and the New acknowledge the great work of God in saving them through the work of the Savior, Jesus. The last two chapters of the Bible picture heaven. John saw the tree of life, growing there as it did in the Garden of Eden, and streams of clear water flowing out from under the throne and watering the land. There is no night there, or death or weeping. And the curse God placed on the world back in the Garden of Eden is gone. This is a perfect place, where God's people enjoy his loving presence into eternity.

Bible Basics

The first two chapters of the Bible picture a perfect earth, where God lived in peace with his people. And the last two chapters of the Bible picture the same. In between lies the story of how God restored this world to its original condition through the work of his Son. It is the greatest story ever told.

Among Jesus' last words to John in the book of Revelation are these: "These words are trustworthy and true. . . . Behold, I am coming soon!". . . John concludes, and we agree, "Amen. Come, Lord Jesus. The grace of the Lord Jesus be with God's people. Amen" (Revelation 22:6,7,20,21).

LEARNING TO PROPERLY INTERPRET AND APPLY THE BIBLE 5

I can still see the concern on Carmen's face. There she sat in my study with her fiancé, Paul, for premarriage counseling—a vivacious young couple in their mid 20s. Growing up, she hadn't been taught much of the Bible. His father had been a Lutheran pastor, but when his father died early, Paul quit going to church. He had been out of church for a while. But now that they were getting married, he brought Carmen back to his roots. During our premarriage counseling, I invited them to join our newly formed Basic Christian Doctrine class. Here's how Carmen reacted: "I will come to your class, Pastor, but I have to tell you that I am a little afraid. You see, I haven't learned that much of the Bible from anyone. So you could teach me anything you wanted and I wouldn't know enough to be able to tell if what you are saying is the truth or not." She was much wiser than she realized. Knowing what you don't know is wisdom.

A lot of people are teaching the Bible these days. And that's a good thing. However, just as with any other subject, the Bible can be taught incorrectly. When its proper message is not understood, it can have disastrous results. Think of how many Jehovah's Witnesses have refused blood transfusions and died because in the Old Testament God told his people not to drink the blood of sacrificial animals. My brother had a high school friend who died of epilepsy because his church taught him that the Bible said he could be healed by his pastor if he had enough faith. He quit taking his medicine and died of a seizure in his college dorm room. But the worst damage that comes from misinterpreting the Bible occurs when wrong teaching destroys someone's faith in their Savior, Jesus Christ. Then they lose their eternal salvation. Sadly, all over the world droves of Bible teachers are misinterpreting the Scriptures to the eternal demise of their students. Carmen had a reason to be cautious, didn't she?

But don't let all this scare you. The Bible is clear enough, and you can learn to read it in an honest way in order to receive its life-giving message. Whenever you read the Bible, just be like Carmen. Be honest about what you do not know. Then learn to ask the right questions in order to find out what you need to know.

In the rest of this chapter, I am going to teach you the right questions to ask every time you read your Bible. This will help you interpret God's Word correctly, and you will grow to become more and more spiritually healthy.

What Did the Passage Mean to the Original Author and His Readers?

The technical term for "how to interpret the Bible" is *hermeneutics* (her-men-oo-tics). One excellent study on how to interpret the Bible is *Biblical Interpretation: The Only Right Way* by David Kuske. You may want to consult this book to learn more about interpreting the Bible.

In this book, we will focus on three of the most important points of interpretation. If you understand these three points and put them into practice, you will do a pretty good job of interpreting Scripture properly. Every time you open your Bible and start reading, you should ask yourself three questions: First, what is the historical context of this passage? Second, what is the literary context of this passage? Third, what light do other sections of Scripture shed on this passage?

Let's spend some time understanding these three questions. As you will see, the answers are quite basic and are in line with common sense.

The Historical Context

Nothing is written in a vacuum. Each time you open your Bible you are visiting a specific time in history. You are at a specific place where God gave a specific message to a specific audience by using a specific writer. We call this the *historical context*. You also know that God's message to that original audience contains timeless truths for all believers of all time. As you study the Bible, your task is to discover the specific message God gave to the original readers in its historical context and then discover the specific application it has to your own life of faith.

Let me give you a simple example of the importance of the historical setting of a sentence. If I said to you "The pig flew right by me!" what would I mean? Well, if I were watching a Walt Disney film, I would mean that a cartoon character of a pig flew across the screen. If I were at an iron ore smelting plant that had an explosion, I would mean that a piece of iron ingot flew dangerously close to me. If I were watching a greased-pig-catching contest at a fair, I would mean that a real greased-up pig ran right by me. And, finally, if I were a rebellious teenager, I might mean that a police car came whizzing by me on the road. See? Every context yielded a very different meaning. Most of the time when you are studying the Bible there are not as many possible meanings as there were for my example, but we still have to carefully find out the context to any passage in order to understand exactly what God is saying there.

If I read John 3:16, which says, "God so loved the world that he gave his one and only Son, that whoever believes in him shall not perish but have eternal life," the historical context shows that it is a general statement that was spoken to all people of all time. But if I read Psalm 51:18,19, which says, "In your good pleasure make Zion prosper; build up the walls of Jerusalem. Then there will be righteous sacrifices, whole burnt offerings to delight you; then bulls will be offered on your altar," I realize that I will want to explore the historical context to find out what the psalmist is talking about and whether the verse applies to me in the New Testament period or not.

At this point you might be saying to yourself, "But I don't know much about history. How can I know the historical context of a passage?" Don't worry. The Bible supplies us with everything we need to understand the historical context. It's not what we bring to the Bible, but what the Bible gives to us that counts. In other words, if you were on a desert island with nothing but the Bible, you would have all you need to study it.

Here is a biblical example of how wrong notions can come from ignoring the context around a passage. There are many churches that say that God wants Christians to give at least 10 percent of their income to the church for gospel ministry. They will even go so far as to say that if you do not give 10 percent, you are sinning. Where does this number come from? It comes from the laws God gave the Israelites through Moses in the book of Exodus. It was how the Israelites were to support their priests, who were not allowed to work a regular job. We must realize that God's Old Testament laws were made obsolete when Jesus, the true temple of God and the ultimate High Priest, came to earth. The Old Testament temple was destroyed, and the temple priesthood was phased out. God does not tell Christians anywhere in the Bible that they must give a certain percent to gospel ministry. He actually wants Christians to dedicate their whole lives to Jesus, who lived his whole life for them. Then after they have dedicated everything to God, they are to prayerfully serve God by using some of their money for family needs, some for taxes, some for gospel ministry, and some for the less fortunate. We are free to give as the Lord leads us to give. Without an understanding of the historical context of the laws about tithing, and how those laws were set aside in the New Testament, Christians would bind themselves to a law to which God has not bound us.

The Literary Context

There is another question we must ask. What is the *literary context* of a passage? Just as every passage has a historical context, so every passage has a literary context. The literary context of a passage has to do with the nature of the passage itself and where it is found in Scripture. Every passage is written in a certain style, for example, narrative or prose. Every passage is either part of the Old Testament or the New Testament. It is found in a certain book, in a certain chapter, and within that chapter it has certain ideas that come before it and that follow it. It is usually part of a bigger story or discussion. You can easily misunderstand a passage if you overlook its literary context.

Don't think this is beyond your ability. You don't have to have a PhD in English to figure out the literary context. While you will sometimes need help from a book or from your pastor, you can usually start with what you already know. You know that when you read the sports page in a newspaper, for example, you are going to treat the lead article differently than you might a poem where someone is describing a game in figurative language. And you are going to approach the page where readers express their opinions differently than you are going treat the statistical analyses of all the games played yesterday. Figurative language, hard-core statistics, running narrative, personal opinion—these are all different literary contexts. You know how to handle them on the sports page, and in much the same way, you know how to handle them when reading the Bible.

Allow one example of how the literary context helps us properly understand a passage. In Isaiah 65:20, Isaiah speaks about heaven in very earthly terms. Here is what he says:

> Never again will there be in it
> > an infant who lives but a few days,
> > or an old man who does not live out his years;
> he who dies at a hundred
> > will be thought a mere youth;
> he who fails to reach a hundred
> > will be considered accursed.

I once overheard a Christian discussing this verse with his pastor, "Why does Isaiah say that in heaven it will be unusual for a person to die as young as a hundred? I thought we would never die there." That's a good question. To answer it you have to consider the style of literature found in the prophets. It is prophecy, written in poetic form. Sometimes the prophets take poetic license and use pictures to make points that are not to be taken literally. No one dies in heaven. That is clear from many other Scripture passages that speak directly about heaven. So, Isaiah does not mean that people will live a long time in heaven and eventually die, because the rest of Scripture rules out death in heaven. So we simply accept Isaiah's use of a poetic form. He is using earthly terms to say that heaven will not be anything like the earth. It will be far different, far better.

Always Let Scripture Interpret Scripture

Maybe now you are asking the question, "This still sounds hard. How do I know when the prophet literally means what he says or is just using an earthly picture? Like when Micah says that the future ruler of Israel will be born in Bethlehem, how do I know if Bethlehem is a figurative place or the real town of Bethlehem?" That's a good question. The best answer is that you should always let Scripture interpret Scripture. Regarding the Isaiah passage above, there are many other clearer passages about heaven that will help you separate poetic license from the straight facts of the prophecy. The Bible clearly tells us that there will be no death in heaven, so we know Isaiah is speaking figuratively. Regarding the Micah prophecy, the New Testament interprets it to refer to the literal town of Bethlehem, so we can be quite sure that Micah is not talking about a figurative Bethlehem.

So when you come across a passage that seems confusing, slow down, keep in mind the historical and literary contexts of the passages, and then search all the other passages you can find that speak on that subject.

Letting Scripture interpret Scripture is a key truth on which the Lutheran church is built. It is in contrast to using the writings of human beings to determine the meaning of Scripture. It is in contrast to forcing Scripture into the mold of human logic, saying that if some point doesn't make sense to human logic, it cannot be right, even though the Bible says it.

The Scriptures themselves are the tool to help you understand the passage you are studying. A little later we will suggest some more tools you might use to do this kind of scriptural study.

Practice Interpreting the Bible

Now that you know to look for the *historical* and *literary contexts* and to *let Scripture interpret Scripture*, let's apply this to a section of the Bible.

Let me tell you another story. It's about Dan and his struggle with one of the more difficult passages of Scripture tucked away in the Old Testament book of Judges. Dan wanted to use Scripture to grow in faith, which is always the reason we study Scripture. Dan came to see me one afternoon. He was very frustrated. He wanted to trust God and his Word, and he knew he needed the Bible to guide him in his life. But he couldn't get past one particular Bible story that in his mind was casting a veil over God's love.

He remembered reading in the book of Judges that a man in Israel named Jephthah had sacrificed his own daughter to God when God had helped him win a battle. Here's what Dan said: "I don't like the God of the Old Testament because any god that demands a man sacrifice his own daughter isn't going to be my god." By the way, Dan was in the military, and he and his wife have two daughters. Take a look at the passage Dan had read.

> Jephthah made a vow to the LORD: "If you give the Ammonites into my hands, whatever comes out of the door of my house to meet me when I return in triumph from the Ammonites will be the LORD's, and I will sacrifice it as a burnt offering."
>
> Then Jephthah went over to fight the Ammonites, and the LORD gave them into his hands. He devastated twenty towns from Aroer to the vicinity of Minnith, as far as Abel Keramim. Thus Israel subdued Ammon.
>
> When Jephthah returned to his home in Mizpah, who should come out to meet him but his daughter, dancing to the sound of tambourines! She was an only child. Except for her he had neither son nor daughter. When he saw her, he tore his clothes and cried, "Oh! My daughter! You have made me miserable and wretched, because I have made a vow to the LORD that I cannot break."
>
> "My father," she replied, "you have given your word to the LORD. Do to me just as you promised, now that the LORD has avenged you of your enemies, the Ammonites. But grant me this one request," she said. "Give me two months to roam the hills and weep with my friends, because I will never marry."
>
> "You may go," he said. And he let her go for two months. She and the girls went into the hills and wept because she would

never marry. After the two months, she returned to her father and he did to her as he had vowed. And she was a virgin.

From this comes the Israelite custom that each year the young women of Israel go out for four days to commemorate the daughter of Jephthah the Gileadite. (Judges 11:30-40)

Now that you have read the passage, tell me, was Dan right? Did God demand that Jephthah sacrifice his daughter? If so, Dan had a good point. I wouldn't want to worship a God who demanded child sacrifice. Let's ask our leading questions: What is the historical and literary context of the passage? And how does the rest of Scripture help us understand this passage?

The passage comes from the book of Judges. Judges is history. We do not have to deal with Hebrew poetry or figurative language. The literary context is straight narrative. The historical context is a very dark time in Israel's history. The period of the judges comes between Joshua, who conquered the Promised Land about 1400 B.C., and the period of the kings, which started about 1000 B.C. During this time the Israelites did many evil things. The author wanted to tell about a very real event in Israel's history. He wanted to show how dark these times really were.

The passage is about a mistake that one man made, both in making a bad vow and then forcing himself to keep it even though he committed another sin in the process. Before the section about Jephthah's vow, we get a glimpse of the man himself. In Judges 11:1-3 we are told:

Jephthah the Gileadite was a mighty warrior. His father was Gilead; his mother was a prostitute. Gilead's wife also bore him sons, and when they were grown up, they drove Jephthah away. "You are not going to get any inheritance in our family," they said, "because you are the son of another woman." So Jephthah fled from his brothers and settled in the land of Tob, where a group of adventurers gathered around him and followed him.

Jephthah was chosen by God to be a judge in Israel. Yet he grew up outside the nation of Israel and may not have had the chance to learn many of God's laws or to grow in faith and discernment. He was probably lacking in spiritual maturity. The fact that God used Jephthah to deliver his people does not make Jephthah immune to sin. Nor do his sins make him an unbeliever. When we look at the broader historical context of Judges, we see men like Samson, whose life was hardly a model for us to follow. But in spite of his sins and weaknesses, Samson knew the Lord and could pray to him for help. We also see Gideon, who delivered the Israelites but then later did something that caused the Israelites to fall into the sin of idolatry (Judges 8:27). From this larger context we learn that God's judges, who lived during a dark period of Israel's history, were children of their times and were often spiritually immature and did things God did not condone. But God still used them to bless Israel. Interestingly, this story also shows the obedience and integrity of Jephthah's daughter, who like most Israelite women considered marriage and child rearing a blessing from God.

Let's ask the question again. Was Dan correct? Was the God of the Old Testament a ruthless god who demanded that Jephthah sacrifice his daughter? Not at all! Jephthah was an Israelite who made a rash vow and wrongly kept it. He did not have to make the vow in the first place, and he could have easily asked advice from a prophet or a priest (assuming he could have found one) after he realized his daughter would be the one who would have to die.

Finally, when we look at what the rest of Scripture says about child sacrifice, we realize that God never condoned such a thing. In Jeremiah 19:5, the prophet conveyed God's rebuke to the Israelites who practiced child sacrifice: "They have built the high places of Baal to burn their sons in the fire as offerings to Baal—something I did not command or mention, nor did it enter my mind." So this and other passages in Scripture tell us that God never wanted his people to do such a thing. It is clear that he never asked Jephthah to make his vow, nor did he approve of his killing his daughter.

So what happened to Dan? Well, I explained the context of the story to him, and he agreed that he had misunderstood the meaning of that story. He had not considered the historical and literary context. Nor had he taken the time to search the rest of Scripture to see what it has to say on the matter. Today Dan is a sincere Bible student who has learned to study God's Word carefully and deliberately.

How Does This Passage Apply to My Life Today?

In the example above, Dan was trying to apply Scripture to his life, but he ran into a roadblock that was keeping him from loving his heavenly Father. Nevertheless, he was trying to do something that every Christian should do, namely, read Scripture in order to grow in faith. Never study the Bible simply to acquire knowledge. Always study the Bible to grow in your faith. As you read, always ask yourself: How does this passage apply to my life today?

The Bible was written to instruct us. But not all Scripture instructs us in the same way. Some sections of Scripture tell us directly what the Lord wants all Christians to believe and do. Other sections are written to a specific group of people, for example, the churches to whom Paul wrote. We then must ask how his words apply to us. Some parts of the letters are clearly directed to all believers of all times. Other parts of those letters address special needs of the congregation, and we must sometimes work hard to apply what Paul said to the recipients of the letter in a way that fits Christians in general.

Other sections of Scripture are narratives. The story of Jephthah is a narrative. The thing to remember about narratives is that they simply tell us what happened. Some narratives tell us what God was doing to bless his people. The Old Testament story of Joseph, for example, tells us how God saved the descendants of Abraham from death through starvation and in the process kept his promise of a Savior alive. It also tells us about a God-fearing and wise man, Joseph. Watching Joseph show love to his brothers and listening to what he says teaches us how the Lord wants us to act. God wants us to love him above all things, leave matters in his hand, and live before him in wisdom and humility. Joseph gives us a pattern to follow. In the context of God's clear words in other parts of Scripture that instruct us on how to live, such stories give us concrete examples that we can take to heart and try to imitate.

Let's return to the story of Jephthah. We can mine this story for any number of truths. One truth is that God spared his people, the Israelites, from the destruction of their enemies by sending

Jephthah to deliver them. In sparing his people, God protected the line of our Savior. I can observe this and thank the Lord for watching over his people in dark times so that the light of God's salvation can now shine on me. And, regardless of any of the other details of the story, this example of God's faithfulness in the past helps me trust that in the future he will always be faithful to his promises to me. It also teaches me that God can work through sinful human beings like me. I never condone my sin or think of it lightly, but I know that if I fall, God's work of building his church through his Word will continue. I also learn the sad results of spiritual immaturity. Jephthah made a vow to the Lord, which was not wrong, and he carried through with his vow, which in most cases is exactly what the Lord would have had him do. But Jephthah's immaturity caused him to make a foolish vow and then wrongly follow through with it.

Comparing Joseph with Jephthah, we see one man who served God wisely and humbly and was richly blessed and we see another man whose service to God was mixed with foolish and wrong behavior and see how greatly he suffered for it. Through this we learn how important it is to immerse ourselves in God's Word and pray for wisdom and guidance in our lives. We also see an example of how one person's sins affect the lives of other people. Jephthah's daughter seems to have had more spiritual maturity than her father. She wanted to obey him. She wanted to fulfill her God-given role to marry and have children to God's glory. She obeyed her father and mourned her inability to carry out God's wishes for life. How sad! We learn to pray, "Lord, help us never lead one of your people into sin or keep them from the blessings you intend for them to have." So we take this narrative of Scripture, interpret it in the light of the many clear passages of Scripture that speak about similar themes, and we let the story teach us.

Bible Study Resources

Are there any tools that can help a Christian study Scripture? Yes! Here's a look at some of them.

Teachers

Any Christian can go into God's Word, interpret it correctly, and learn to apply it to his or her life. But the Lord has always supplied his people with teachers. Teachers have been blessed by the Lord with the time and opportunity to study God's Word in depth. They have sat at the feet of other teachers who have taught them. The Bible also says that God has given the spiritual gifts of knowledge and teaching to some people in his church, and the Lord wants to use these people to guide his followers to spiritual maturity. Some of your teachers will be pastors with whom you can speak face-to-face. Others have written books, to which you can turn at any time. But never let those resources become more important than Scripture itself. The last thing you want to do is fall in love with resources and neglect reading the Bible itself. Read the Bible, and let the resources help you when you have questions.

Study Bibles

One good, basic resource is a study Bible. Most study Bibles have an introduction for every book of the Bible. In each introduction you will find comments about the date, the place, and the setting of the book; notes about the author and the original readers; the occasion for writing the book; and a general outline. It is very helpful to read the introduction before reading any portion of a book in order to get the historical context of what you are reading. Another helpful feature of a study Bible is that it usually has notes along the bottom of the page that coincide with the verses above. Often in those notes are comments pertinent to the historical and the literary context of the passages you are reading. Some study Bibles give a lot of life application insights as well. These can be helpful in learning to apply Scripture to your own life.

Some words of caution: Always remember that the notes in a study Bible are not inspired by God. Sometimes you will want to challenge them. Most study Bibles are written by non-Lutheran authors. Some study Bibles have so many theological errors that they are a waste of your money. Before you spend your money on a study Bible, ask your pastor for his advice. If someone gives you one as a gift, be very careful on how you use it. Many of the notes will be accurate and helpful. Some will not.

Many Christians bring their study Bibles to their church's group Bible studies. If you do, compare what your pastor says with what the study Bible says. Try not to use your study Bible to answer his questions or to dispute points he is making. If you see a discrepancy between his comments and those in the study Bible's notes, ask him for clarification. Such interaction will help you better understand the section you are studying and also give you a better feel for where your study Bible will be helpful and where it might not.

Commentaries

Another very helpful resource is a commentary. A commentary is a book written about a book of the Bible. Just like in a study Bible, a commentary will start with an introduction to the book you are reading. That introduction will give you a lot of help with understanding the historical context of the book. Then the commentary will work methodically through the book, verse by verse, giving you short sections of Scripture interspersed with comments from the author. Those who have written commentaries have spent a lot of time studying and teaching each book they are presenting. You can gather many rich and meaningful insights from a commentary. But you still have to bear in mind that their comments are not inspired. Sometimes you might want to compare what one commentator says with what another says. Northwestern Publishing House has produced a good series of commentaries on the entire Bible called The People's Bible. These commentaries are available at a reasonable cost and will bring the knowledge and spiritual insights of many pastors and teachers to bear on your Bible study. These commentaries are easy to read, very informative, and accurately teach the Scriptures.

Bible Encyclopedias, Handbooks, and Dictionaries

Another good Bible companion is a Bible encyclopedia. A Bible encyclopedia lists topics from the Bible in alphabetical order. A Bible encyclopedia contains articles, pictures, maps, and charts that have to do with your subject. Some are one-volume books. Others are larger three- to five-volume sets. Get what you can afford.

Bible handbooks are different from Bible encyclopedias. They usually go through the Bible in order book by book. They are often a single volume. They feature graphics—pictures and charts.

You might also find a Bible dictionary to be very helpful. A Bible dictionary is similar to a Bible encyclopedia but will have simple definitions and descriptions of persons, places, and things, rather than long articles about various Bible subjects. I would get a Bible encyclopedia before I got a Bible dictionary.

If you are thinking about buying one of these Bible study helps, talk with your pastor. It is likely that he will have some in his library that you can look at or perhaps borrow for a short time.

Concordances

A concordance is one of the most powerful tools for Bible study. Many pastors and teachers use a concordance more than any other Bible study tool. There is no reason anyone cannot learn to use one. They are quite straightforward and easy to use.

Let me give you an example of how you might use one. The other day someone said to me, "The Bible doesn't really emphasize Baptism that much, so why is it so important to you?" How would you answer that challenge? Where would you go to find the verses on Baptism? Here is where a concordance comes in handy. A concordance is a list of all the words found in the Bible. The words are listed in alphabetical order along with references to the passages in which they can be found. Each reference is accompanied by a few words from the passage. Here is an example of what you would find under the word *baptism* in a concordance. (The *b* stands for "baptism.")

Baptism
Mt 21:25 John's *b*—where did it come from?
Mk 1:4 and preaching a *b* of repentance
Mk 10:38 baptized with the *b* I am baptized

In my concordance there are 19 passages listed under *baptism* and more listed under the words *baptize, baptized,* and *baptizing.* In order to answer the challenge that the Bible does not emphasize Baptism, all I needed to do was read these passages about Baptism and check the context in which they are found. I quickly found that Baptism had a very prominent place in the teachings of John the Baptist, Jesus, and the apostles.

People also use concordances to find a passage they remember reading, but cannot remember where they read it. If you can remember any word from the passage, you can look up that word in your concordance and then read all the passage fragments listed below the word. You will likely find the passage you are thinking about.

Concordances are found in the backs of some Bibles, but they are not complete concordances. So sometimes you have to look up several words before finding the right passage. Concordances with every word found in Scripture are called exhaustive, or complete, concordances. You can purchase these from Northwestern Publishing House or any Christian bookstore. An exhaustive concordance will list every word of the Bible.

Related to a concordance is a topical index. Some Bibles, especially study Bibles, have them. Let's say you want to read up on the biblical use of the word *righteousness.* A topical index would give you several references from the Old and New Testaments. In my study Bible, the topical index will even tell me where the word is discussed in some of the notes, maps, and charts throughout the Bible.

Electronic Resources

Computer Bible study programs are quite popular today. They range from high-end programs that contain Bible dictionaries and the ability to search the Bible in many languages to basic programs designed for home use. The strength of all computer Bible study programs is their ability to quickly do word searches and display Bible verses. In other words, they serve as electronic concordances. Usually, you merely type in a word and the program will display the results in a format like a book concordance. The programs usually allow you to click on the verse in the concordance window and see the whole verse in another window. This saves the time of looking up each passage in your Bible. For example, in just a few minutes you can read every passage of Scripture in which the word *baptism* occurs.

These programs have other features that can help you study the Bible. Northwestern Publishing House is putting many of its books in Logos electronic format. This allows you to search these books in the same way as you search the Bible. For example, you can search *baptism* and find articles in books about that topic. It is best to do some research into the features of these programs before you purchase one. But if all you need is a Bible concordance, any one of the several programs available will work.

Pulling It All Together

Let's pull together everything we have learned. First, get your bearings on the historical context of the passage you are studying. Ask yourself what the historical context might mean for your understanding of the passage. If nothing readily comes to mind, continue working with the passage, keeping the historical context in mind. As your study progresses, it might become clear that the historical background plays into the interpretation of the Bible more than you thought at first.

Second, ask yourself, "What kind of literature is this?" Is the section narrative, poetry, a parable, a letter, or prophecy? After you have considered what style of writing you are reading, study the train of thought that comes before and after your passage. It is helpful to read the whole book in which the passage is found. But if you don't have the time, then scan the whole book, but be sure to read the chapter right before and after your passage. Then read more carefully the paragraphs directly before and after your passage. You will start to notice a train of thought that will help put your passage in its proper context. Then reread your passage, looking for figures of speech and repeating phrases.

As you begin to think about the meaning of the passage, before that meaning is set in concrete in your thinking, search out related sections in the Bible. What light do these other passages shed on your ideas? If your passage contains names and places, a Bible dictionary or Bible handbook might be helpful. If it contains theological truths, you might want to consult a good basic book on Christian doctrine to help you sort out the issue. If you still have questions about certain things in the passage, this is good time to read a basic commentary or ask your pastor.

You might try to write in your own words what the passage is saying. Reread the passage in the Bible, and compare it to what you have written down. See if they sound the same.

Once you have followed these careful methods, you will be much more satisfied that you have begun to understand what the passage is saying. It never hurts to consult a good commentary after you have studied the passage your own. Also remember the importance of God's gift of pastors and teachers.

Prayer and Bible study go together too. Before approaching a passage, stop to pray. Ask God to open your mind to understand what the passage says, and then ask him to help you apply that passage to your life. Ask him to soften your heart to help you accept his Word. God loves to answer prayers like these. When you make such requests of God, in essence you are praying, "Your kingdom come," as we do in the Lord's Prayer.

Questions for Studying Scripture

Here is a list of questions you might want to ask as you study Scripture.

A. What is the historical context of the passage?
1. Who wrote this passage?
2. When did he write this passage?
3. To whom did he write this passage?
4. Why did he write this passage?

B. **What is the literary context of the passage?**
   1. Is this passage found in the Old or New Testament?
   2. Where does this passage occur in the book?
   3. What comes right before this passage?
   4. What comes right after this passage?
   5. What type of literature is this passage?

C. **How does this passage apply to my life today?**
   1. What is the timeless truth for all people in this passage?
   2. Does this passage tell me what God has done for me or what I should do for God?
   3. What changes do I need to make in my life because of what this passage says?
   4. What prayer does this passage lead me to say right now?

Styles of Literature Found in the Bible

Introduction

For a moment, consider how many different styles of writing you might read in a day. There are letters, e-mails, memos, textbooks, newspaper articles, sports statistics, editorials, poetry, novels, biographies, road signs, cell phone texts, and now tweets. Each one of those styles has different characteristics, and as you read them, different things go through your mind. You just cannot read a text on a cell phone with the same expectations as you would have for a novel. A text message contains abbreviations that you interpret on the fly. A novel entails a sometimes intricate plot that you try to keep in mind as you move from chapter to chapter.

The Bible contains several different types of literature too. If you don't take this into account, you can get frustrated, or worse, you might completely misunderstand the meaning. We have already referred to the various styles of literature in the Bible. Here are more detailed introductions to the different types of literature in the Bible with some advice on how to read each one.

Historical Narrative

Twenty-two books of the Bible are primarily made up of historical narrative, the first seventeen books of the Old Testament and the first five books of the New Testament. In a narrative, the author is telling a story about something that happened. He is not writing figuratively but literally. In the biblical narratives, you will often find miraculous events. In the Old Testament, God created the world in six, 24-hour days. Elijah went to heaven in a fiery chariot. Jonah got swallowed by a big fish and survived a three-day ordeal in its belly. In the New Testament, Jesus cast out demons and walked on water. He was born of a virgin and rose from the dead on Easter Sunday. All of these miracles defy our logic, but they still happened. They are written as historical narrative.

Many view these historical narratives as something like fantasy novels with hidden allegorical meanings. They discount the miracles themselves as being untrue, and they look for deeper "theological" meanings behind the stories. But don't follow that approach. God is the maker of all things, and he has done many miraculous things in history. He doesn't want us to redefine his-story because some people claim that such things cannot happen.

Narratives are also meant to tell important stories, and in general, the stories do not directly tell us what to believe or do. Yet the accounts of Scripture provide examples of people who held on to God's promises and shaped their lives around them, and the accounts show how God blessed them. Scripture also contains accounts of people who despised God, and we are warned by the outcome of their lives. For instance, when you see David's confidence in God when he stood before the giant Goliath, you can learn to have the same confidence when you face seemingly insurmountable problems. If you are tempted to have Goliath's pride, you can also read what happened to him in the end. In Romans 15:4, the Lord tells us to read the narratives this way: "Everything that was written in the past was written to teach us, so that through endurance and the encouragement of the Scriptures we might have hope."

While narratives give us hope and insight, we cannot say that everything we see in a story somehow tells us how we should live out our own lives. For instance, in the book of Judges, Samson wanted to marry a Philistine woman, something strictly forbidden by the Old Testament law of God. His parents were beside themselves because he wanted to marry a non-Israelite woman. But the writer says, "His parents did not know that this was from the LORD, who was seeking an occasion to confront the Philistines" (Judges 14:4). We would not handle this passage correctly if we surmised that God is telling us to date unbelievers indiscriminately because he might be using us to save their souls. That is taking too much from that narrative and forgetting about other narratives that describe how Israelite men were led astray in their faith by marrying women who served idols.

There is another feature of biblical narrative that ought to be mentioned. Many of the biblical narratives are sermonic. What I mean is that the writer recorded actual events, but with a bent on helping you see some specific truth. Genesis chapter 1 is written this way. God inspired Moses to write a history of the creation of the world in such a way that we learn important theological truths. One truth is that God created everything by the power of his word in six normal days. That's why after every day Moses wrote, "There was evening, and there was morning," which is how the Jewish people described the beginning and end of a 24-hour day.

Other examples of sermonic narrative are the four gospels. Each of them is a biography of the life of Jesus Christ. But they are not written as straight history. Five percent of their words cover about 30 years of Jesus' life. Sixty percent of their words cover three years of his life. Thirty-five percent cover one week of his life. The inordinate amount of attention given to Jesus' ministry and the last week of his life teaches us that the main point of Jesus' life is that he lived, suffered, died, and rose again to save us. Jesus lived for that purpose, and so the stories about his life preach it.

Poetry (Wisdom Literature and Prophecy)

There are 22 Old Testament books that are written in Hebrew poetic style. They are Job, Psalms, Proverbs, Ecclesiastes, Song of Songs, and the 17 prophetic books.

Hebrew poetry uses different techniques than English poetry to emphasize its message. English poetry uses rhyme and meter. Hebrew poetry depends more on structure. It uses parallelism. In Proverbs there are many verses where the first line presents a thought that the second line repeats, or parallels, in a different way. Sometimes the thoughts are opposites, and other times one thought builds on another.

Hebrew poetry also uses repetition. For instance, in Psalm 136 every verse ends with the phrase: "His love endures forever." Originally this psalm was meant to be sung antiphonally between a leader and a choir or congregation. The choir or congregation repeated the refrain many times, which reminded everyone of God's everlasting love.

Hebrew poetry also uses "structural engineering." The structure of the piece often plays a significant role in the meaning of it. One type of structural engineering is centering. The author puts the most important point in the center of his work. A classic example is found in Lamentations. The book is mostly about God's judgment on Israel and the fall of Jerusalem. But right in the middle verses of the middle section of this prophecy, Jeremiah wrote these comforting words: "He does not willingly bring affliction or grief to the children of men" (3:33). God would discipline the Israelites, but he would also someday bless them again.

Another use of structural engineering in Hebrew poetry is the use of acrostics. The most common biblical acrostic is where the first word of each line begins with a different letter of the Hebrew alphabet. Psalm 119 is an acrostic. It has 22 stanzas that have eight lines each. Each set of eight lines begins with the same letter of the Hebrew alphabet. The author is emphasizing the completeness of God's Word by using the complete Hebrew alphabet to describe the Word and its power in his life. Other acrostics are Psalms 25; 34; 37; and 145; and Proverbs 31:10-31.

Hebrew poetry can be some of the most difficult literature to understand, especially when it is found in the writings of the prophets. It is always a good practice to find a trusted commentary and lean on it heavily when needed.

Prophecy

Biblical prophecy is unique in that it does not always speak about the future. Basically, to *prophesy* means to "tell someone what's on God's mind, either about the past, the present, or the future." So it's not always "foretelling" things.

Having said that, we must also point out that the prophets did predict the future. Some prophecy tells the future in a direct way. That is, it says specifically that such and such a thing will come to pass. Other prophecies tell the future in an indirect way. The prophets point to people, places, or events and say that they picture events coming in the future or they are part of God's plan of salvation that finds its fulfillment in Jesus. First Chronicles 17:10-14 is a good example. Nathan, a prophet, told David that one of David's sons would establish his throne forever. This prophecy was partially fulfilled in David's son Solomon, but it was completely and finally fulfilled in Jesus Christ, the great "Son of David."

Also, the prophets often saw the future in two dimensions, as we do when we see a painting or view a mountain range in the distance. We see the width and the height, but we have a hard time telling just how deep it is. We cannot tell how close the foothills are to the majestic peaks in the background. The prophets created their paintings with words. Often they did not even try to create a sense of depth in their writings. Two events are predicted one after another, side by side, but there is no hint that hundreds of years separate the two.

This is what stumped John the Baptist (Matthew 11:2,3). He expected the ministry of Jesus to be followed quickly by judgment day. After all, that's how the Old Testament prophets seem to describe it. Prophecies about Jesus' life are right next to prophecies about his judgment on the world, but the two events are actually very far apart. In some ways, we see the depth better than the prophets did. There have already been more than two thousand years between Jesus' birth and judgment day, and we are still waiting. In the same vein, it is futile to try to predict when prophecies still in the future will take place. Bible teachers who do this are wasting their time.

If we compare the Bible to a swimming pool, the prophets are the deep end of the pool. If you are just learning the Bible, spend less time in the prophets and more time in the narratives. But don't be afraid to jump into the prophets. You will find some very comforting passages there that you will be able to understand fairly well. When you have time, check out Isaiah chapter 53.

Letters

Much of the New Testament is made up of letters. There are 21 letters. They start at Romans and end at Jude. The first 13 were written by Paul, and the rest were written by James, Peter, John, and Jude. We don't know the author of Hebrews, but it too is a letter. When studying letters, it is helpful to understand when and to whom they were written. The book of Acts gives the historical background to most of Paul's letters.

The letters possess many timeless truths. They were written to teach, defend, and explain the truth. They also teach pastors and church members how to live as God's people and extend his kingdom. Most often the timeless truths are to be taken straight out of the passage. But sometimes the author is applying a timeless truth to a certain historical situation and does not intend that his exact words be followed by everyone in the future. For instance, in I Timothy 5:23, Paul tells Timothy, "Stop drinking only water, and use a little wine because of your stomach and your frequent illnesses." Paul is not saying that every believer should drink wine. He was telling Timothy to drink wine because Timothy had stomach problems and wine was considered good medicine. The timeless truth is that God has given us medicines to help our bodies. We are free to use such medicines in a responsible way. Paul was giving practical advice based on this timeless truth. He was not establishing a timeless truth for all people about how to handle their stomach problems. The more you read the letters, the more you will learn how to distinguish timeless truths from practical applications.

Most letters have a structure and train of thought that are easy to follow. They usually begin with a greeting and end with a blessing. They are usually short enough that you can read them in one sitting. Many of Paul's letters start with theological themes and end with practical applications. A study Bible will often give you an outline of the letter. It's a good practice to review the background and the outline of a biblical letter before reading it.

Parables

Parables are not a major literary style, but they can be troublesome, especially if we try to get too much out of them. A parable is a fabricated story that is intended to teach one main spiritual point. Parables can be found throughout Scripture, but by far most of the parables are found in the four gospels because Jesus often used parables in his teaching. When you read a parable, remember that Jesus is not giving you license to take from the parable whatever you please. He wants you to see his one main point. Nor does Jesus intend for each earthly element of the parable to teach a spiritual truth.

For instance, in the parable of the ten virgins in Matthew 25:1-13, Jesus tells about ten women who have oil lamps. Five bring extra oil with them, and five do not. When the time comes for them to go with the bridegroom, some have run out of oil, while the others have not. Jesus' point is that we should always be ready for his return. Some have said that the oil in the lamps represents the Holy Spirit. But the oil is simply an element in the story. When people press the details, they come up with ideas that cannot be proven and may in fact say something that contradicts the rest of Scripture. Look for the main point, and if Scripture itself indicates that some details have meanings in real life, be content with that.

7 Ways to Approach the Bible

In this chapter I will deal with various ways to read the Bible. Of course, you can read the Bible in any way you choose, but here are some ways other people have found helpful. I will note the benefit of each method and any drawbacks people have discovered.

Read the Entire Bible From Cover to Cover

Since you know that the Bible is God's Word, it is understandable that you would want to read every word of it. Lots of people read the Bible straight through from cover to cover. It has its advantages. First of all, you really get to know the whole story of the Bible. Second, you know that at least once you will have seen every passage. Also, after reading the entire Bible, other sections of the Bible will make better sense. Many of the biblical narratives refer to previous events, and it helps to have already read those stories. The New Testament quotes from and alludes to many Old Testament passages. If you have read the Old Testament already, you will see how deeply rooted the New Testament is in the Old.

But there are also some disadvantages to reading the Bible straight through from cover to cover. First of all, you will hit sections that become tedious reading. As soon as Genesis chapter 5, you will encounter a genealogy. Genealogies can be boring to read. They serve a very important purpose, but holding your attention is not that purpose. If you are reading the Bible straight through, give yourself permission to skim the genealogical sections.

Another disadvantage is that you will spend time in large sections that are difficult to apply to our lives. Some of the ceremonial laws pointed ahead to Jesus Christ and his saving work, but this is not clearly stated when you read them. If you get bogged down in Leviticus, give yourself permission to skim it until you get back to the historical narratives. Then go back and work on mining the treasures that can be found in these sections of Scripture also.

The poetic and prophetic books of the Old Testament can also be like quicksand if you read straight through them. The more you wiggle around in them, the deeper you sink into their repetitive thoughts. So when you read the prophets, make sure to have outlines to get a handle on their structures. Don't give up on them by any means. Those books contain some of the most beautiful gospel promises anywhere in Scripture.

Another disadvantage of reading straight through the Bible is that you neglect other very important passages for long periods of time. If you would read only one chapter of the Old Testament a day, it would be months before you got to the New Testament where you learn about Jesus Christ. Because it is challenging to keep your interest in reading through large sections of ceremonial laws, poetry, or prophecy, and because we don't want to neglect the New Testament, editors have put together some special Bible reading plans that schedule daily readings in both Testaments. Ask your pastor if he can help you locate one of these.

There are also a host of places to find Bible reading plans that will get you through the Bible in one, two, three, four, or five years. You just need to look for them. In Northwestern Publishing House's devotional booklet called *Meditations,* you will find a Bible reading plan that displays a new reading at the bottom of each daily meditation page. The Wisconsin Synod periodical *Forward in Christ* also has a Bible reading plan. There are other such plans available. If you do an Internet search on Bible reading plans, you will find a number of them.

Another way to work through the entire Bible while living a fast-paced life is to buy the Bible on CD and play it in your car during your daily commute. I have known several people who have done this, and I noticed that they grew in their faith dramatically as a result. You can find a host of Bibles on CD by surfing the Internet. Just type "audio Bible" into any Internet search engine. In my opinion, the best audio Bibles are those that dramatize the readings. In a dramatized Bible there are different voices for the different people in each story.

Reading One Book at a Time

Another approach to Bible reading is to choose a book and focus on that one book for while. You could start with one of the shorter books like Ruth, Esther, 1 Peter, or James. First read the book in one sitting without any analytical thinking on your part at all. Just let the words and thoughts of the text settle into your heart and mind. Then look up the background to the book in a study Bible or Bible commentary. Notice who the author is, when it was written, why it was written, and look at an outline of the book. Then reread the book slowly, watching for repeating phrases and the main points the author is making. You might want to write down any verses that seem to jump out at you as you are reading. You can go back to these verses later to review what they are teaching you.

You might consider keeping a running journal of what you notice as you read, and when you are done, read through your notes again. See if there are any recurring themes. Then you might read through the book slowly again and write your own paraphrase as you read it. This will help you process what you are reading. You will be amazed at how the story or train of thought comes alive in your mind as you read, then process, then write what you see there.

After you have written your own paraphrase of the book, reread all the verses on your list of those that jumped out at you. You might start committing those verses to memory. They will mean more to you once they are in your memory, and you will be able to use them and help others use them since now you know and understand them in their context. Then, to really help you make your study of Scripture come alive, choose a family member or friend to tell one of your favorite verses to. As you speak to that person, explain why that verse or section of Scripture has become so important to you. As you share the verse with him or her, it will become a lasting treasure in your life.

If you are studying the Bible book by book, it might be advisable to alternate between books from the Old and New Testaments. That way you will stay current in your understanding of the all the writings before and after Christ.

Studying the Bible to Answer Key Questions

Many people do not open their Bibles unless they have some key questions about certain doctrines or they need help with certain problems they are having. However, it is always better to have a regular habit of reading the Scriptures regardless of whether you have burning questions or problems. That way your growth is not dictated by the occasional struggles of life but rather by the beautiful revelation of Scripture as the Holy Spirit planned to deliver it.

Having said this, it can be very helpful to study the Bible as a reference book. It answers all of life's most important questions. If you are in a discussion with someone about an important teaching of the Bible and the two of you have a disagreement or you are uncertain, you will feel confident when you find out what the Bible has to say.

Studying With a Group

It is important to study the Bible with other Christians. God has brought us together into a community of believers and wants us to use our collective knowledge and spiritual gifts to bless one another. Romans chapter 12, I Corinthians chapter 12, and I Peter chapter 4 give us a host of reasons why it is preferable to study Scripture in groups. If you study with others, you will discover insights that you might never have found alone. One of the best Bible study groups to join is the Sunday morning Bible study at your church. Your pastor can guide you into the depths of God's Word. God wants his people to study his Word together.

A group can be two or more people. Jesus promised, "Where two or three come together in my name, there am I with them" (Matthew 18:20). Small groups have advantages. Sometimes you will feel more free to ask questions and ponder difficult subjects in a smaller group.

Conclusion

I remember hearing two radio personalities talking about all the different ways to exercise. They each shared their preferences. Finally one of them said, "The main thing is just that you get moving." That's the way it is with Bible study. You just need to get moving. There are many different ways to read and study the Bible. But really, all you need to do is pick up your Bible and start reading. Find your own style and try different approaches. Just remember, every time you open your Bible, God is speaking to you personally from his heart to yours. So let him speak to you as often as possible. You may not fully understand everything you are reading, but you will understand some things, and each time you learn something it will help you interpret more difficult passages the next time you read. So just keep reading and learning God's Word.

    I started this little book by comparing the Bible to a swimming pool. I promised to teach you how to "swim" in the Bible. I hope I have succeeded. The Bible is nothing to be afraid of. It is the most wonderful book on the planet, and it is there for you. So dive in, and start enjoying the Water of Life!